"This is the best book available addressing the serious problems that OCD can cause in families. *Loving Someone with OCD* is a uniquely helpful and wonderful book because it provides step-by-step, easily understandable plans for dealing with every problem that commonly arises between OCD sufferers and their loved ones. The format of the book makes developing a successful plan for overcoming family problems a cinch."

—Ian Osborn, MD, *psychiatrist, assistant professor of psychiatry at the University of New Mexico Health Science Center, and author of* Tormenting Thoughts and Secret Rituals: The Hidden Epidemic of Obsessive-Compulsive Disorder

"I am excited to read this book, with its very specific and detailed instructions on how to help a loved one deal with and hopefully recover from his or her OCD. The chapters on designing and implementing family contracts, with their step-by-step directions, should be especially helpful in the day-by-day battle with OCD. This book should also be particularly helpful for those of us who do not have a qualified therapist available for treatment. I recommend that every family with an OCD member—child, sibling, spouse, and so forth—purchase a copy of this workbook. I only wish we had had access to it twenty years ago."

—Jacqueline Stout, *owner of the online support list Parents of Adults with OCD, sixteen-year member of the Obsessive-Compulsive Foundation, and mother of an adult who has had severe OCD for twenty-three years*

"*Loving Someone with OCD* is a long overdue book that provides solid and accurate information along with extremely practical advice for anyone who has a loved one with OCD. This book is a tremendous resource! I am thrilled to be able to provide this to all families of my patients with OCD. If someone you love has OCD, read this book first."

—Mark E. Crawford, Ph.D., *licensed clinical psychologist and author of* The Obsessive-Compulsive Trap

"*Loving Someone with OCD* is unique in the literature on obsessive-compulsive disorder because it is not for the person suffering with the disorder—it's for the family or friends of the sufferer. If you live with or love someone with this problem, this is the one book on the subject you should read. The authors lay out, step-by-step, what a family needs to do to stop supporting the OCD and start supporting the person with OCD while he or she deals with the disorder. This book is the next best thing to bringing a therapist home to live with you."

—*Patricia Perkins, JD, executive director of the Obsessive-Compulsive Foundation, Inc.*

"All too often the families of those suffering from OCD are ignored. *Loving Someone with OCD* goes beyond other books for families of OCD sufferers; rather than simply providing them with understanding, it gives them the tools to help themselves as well as their loved ones."

—*Jonathan B. Grayson, Ph.D., director of the Anxiety and Agoraphobia Treatment Center and assistant clinical professor of psychiatry at Temple University Medical School*

"This excellent book is just what families need when they are stuck in the web of OCD. It goes beyond simply helping families understand what needs to change by offering a practical, step-by-step guide to doing it. Very easy to read—clear and positive—this book will bring hope and help to many in despair."

—*Aureen Pinto Wagner, Ph.D., clinical associate professor of neurology at the University of Rochester School of Medicine and Dentistry, director of the OCD and Anxiety Consultancy in Rochester, NY, and author of* What to do when your Child has OCD, Up and Down the Worry Hill, *and* Treatment of OCD in Children and Adolescents

loving someone with OCD

Help for You & Your Family

KAREN J. LANDSMAN, PH.D.
KATHLEEN M. RUPERTUS, MA, MS
CHERRY PEDRICK, RN

New Harbinger Publications, Inc.

Distributed in Canada by Raincoast Books

Copyright © 2005 by Karen Landsman, Kathleen Rupertus, and Cherry Pedrick
New Harbinger Publications, Inc.
5674 Shattuck Avenue
Oakland, CA 94609

New Harbinger Publications' Web site address: www.newharbinger.com

Cover design by Amy Shoup
Acquired by Catharine Sutker
Text design by Tracy Marie Carlson

ISBN-10: 1-57224-329-5
ISBN-13: 978-1-57224-329-3

All Rights Reserved
Printed in the United States of America

FSC
Mixed Sources
Product group from well-managed
forests and other controlled sources

Cert no. SW-COC-002283
www.fsc.org
© 1996 Forest Stewardship Council

Library of Congress Cataloging-in-Publication Data

Landsman, Karen J.
  Loving someone with OCD : help for you and your family / by Karen J. Landsman, Kathleen M. Rupertus, and Cherry Pedrick.
      p. cm.
  Includes bibliographical references.
  ISBN-13 978-1-57224-329-3
  ISBN-10 1-57224-329-5
  1. Obsessive-compulsive disorder—Popular works. 2. Obsessive-compulsive disorder—Patients—Family relationships. I. Rupertus, Kathleen M. II. Pedrick, Cherry. III. Title.
  RC533.L26 2006
  362.196'85227—dc22
                                            2005009184

Contents

Foreword

The tragedy of psychiatric illnesses such as obsessive-compulsive disorder (OCD) is not just in the suffering of those afflicted but also in the profound impact the symptoms have upon all members of the family living in close contact with the person. Families are frequently pushed to the breaking point by the emotional and physical demands made by persistent obsessive thoughts and unabated compulsive behaviors. It is as if a bully has invaded and occupied the home and then imposed its own tyrannical set of arbitrary rules upon the family. It's not uncommon for family members to be "required" to devote hours per day to cleaning, checking, and reassurance behaviors demanded by the person with OCD. Thousands of dollars may be wasted on replacing objects needlessly discarded as "contaminated" or on cleansers used to clean objects until they are deemed "perfectly safe." The tension that results from the day-to-day demands of the disease and the emotional and physical outbursts between family members create a maladaptive environment that further inflames OCD symptoms.

The book you are about to read represents the cumulative thinking from decades of theory, research, and clinical observations attempting to both describe and understand the patterns of family interaction and functioning under the strain of psychiatric illness such as OCD. The book is illuminated by Karen Landsman's and Kathleen Rupertus's personal experiences as expert clinicians treating OCD using cognitive behavioral principles and by Cherry Pedrick's perspective as a person who has recovered from OCD and whose own family was greatly affected by the disease. The resulting volume presents a highly practical and effective approach that gives concerned family members a road map and strategy for effectively reversing the corrosive effects of day-to-day accommodation to the disease. The approach emphasizes an accurate understanding of OCD and an alliance between family members against the true culprit—the disease of OCD. It fosters improved communication, greater empathy, and cooperation between family members. *Loving Someone with OCD* lays out a collaborative process whereby the family and the person with OCD gradually relinquish automatic accommodation responses to the symptoms and embrace risk taking. By mutually altering the culture of automatic accommodation and keeping the peace, recovery from OCD is possible.

This is a unique book because, while many volumes have been written outlining the basic principles and theories of helping families cope with a mentally ill member, few offer a specific, step-by-step strategy for doing so. A thorough self-examination of your own reactions as a family member to the person with OCD and the symptoms is a large component of the approach. The workbook-style format lends itself to reflection upon maladaptive feelings, attitudes, and reactions that maintain the OCD status quo. This book guides the reader toward more positive responses that counteract the rampant emotionality that fuels counterproductive (quick-fix) responses which further reinforce and imbed OCD symptoms. The persistent overfocus of family members upon the person with OCD and "fixing the problem" fosters a state of neglect of your own mental, physical, and spiritual well-being, which leads to mental burnout, fatigue, and depression. The authors emphasize strengthening individual resilience by finding a healthier balance between self-care and focus on the problem.

While not a substitute for treatment from a qualified mental-health professional trained in the treatment of OCD and families, this book can be safely utilized as a first step toward change. People who are already receiving cognitive behavioral therapy for OCD can use the ideas in the book to further effect changes in home environments that have not been optimally supportive of recovery efforts.

Perhaps the most valuable aspect of the book is the message of hope that unmistakably reverberates through its pages. Family members can make an important difference in affecting the course and outcome of treatment for OCD in a family member. This book provides the knowledge and tools that can be valuable to any family member seeking to support the healing process in his or her loved one. Through careful and conscientious attention to the many pearls contained within this book, combined with qualified professional assistance, family members can successfully reclaim their family from the grip of the OCD.

—Bruce M. Hyman, Ph.D., LCSW
    Director, OCD Resource Center of Florida
    Hollywood, Florida
    www.ocdhope.com

Karen J. Landsman, Ph.D.: I would like to thank my colleagues and mentors at The Anxiety and Agoraphobia Treatment Center who continually share with me their tremendous insight and knowledge about OCD treatment and my mentors at The University of Maryland Medical School and University of Maryland College Park who provided me with a strong base from which to grow. My heartfelt thanks belong to my patients for sharing their stories and lives with OCD and trusting me to help them. Kathy and Cherry made writing this book an enjoyable, challenging, and creative experience—thank you very much. Finally, I am most grateful for the support and encouragement of my husband and family.

Kathleen M. Rupertus, MA, MS: I would like to thank Karen and Cherry for their heartfelt efforts in bringing our ideas and experiences to life through this book. They made this endeavor both a pleasure and a memorable learning experience. I am especially grateful to my mentor, Dr. Jonathan Grayson, who has demonstrated his faith and invested his valuable time and efforts in guiding my professional growth. I would also like to express my heartfelt gratitude to my patients and their families who have allowed me to journey with them out of the depths of OCD. I am especially thankful for the blessings, love, and support of my family; most especially that of my husband, Matt, and my children, Sarah, Matthew, and Rebecca. I am most grateful to God, who has allowed me to transform my own struggles with OCD into triumph and who has encouraged me to use this experience to reach out and share with others.

Cherry Pedrick, RN: I am thankful to my husband, Jim, and my son, James, for demonstrating what it means to be truly supportive as I've struggled with OCD. It has been an honor to help Karen and Kathy share their tremendous expertise with families dealing with OCD. Most of all, I thank my God for making it all possible.

We are grateful to Bruce Hyman for his encouragement and contribution to this project. We would like to thank Brady, our editor, who helped us clarify our ideas. We also thank Catharine Sutker and all those at New Harbinger for their encouragement, support, and expertise.

Introduction

About 2.5 percent of the population, or 6.6 million people, will develop obsessive-compulsive disorder (OCD) in their lifetime (Niehous and Stein 1997). They aren't the only ones affected. Those numbers jump dramatically when you add family and friends. Obsessive-compulsive disorder affects almost everyone around the person with the disorder. The effects are distinctly different from those of other illnesses. Loved ones, in their desire to help ease the anxiety and distress, are sucked into a lifestyle filled with rituals and avoidance. They often feel boxed into a corner by OCD, almost as much as their loved one who has the disorder.

The main focus of this book is not helping your loved one break free from OCD. That might surprise you! You may have purchased this book for that very reason. The reality is this: you cannot free your loved one; the best therapist in the world cannot free your loved one from OCD. You can help and the right therapy can help, but your loved one will play the most important role in breaking free from OCD. The principal focus of this book is helping you take care of yourself and your family. You'll learn to make changes that will help you break free from the tyranny of OCD. These changes will make it more difficult for your loved one to stay bound by OCD. If your loved one is not pursuing recovery, we'll prepare you to be ready with information as their desire to break free from OCD also grows.

HOW THIS BOOK CAN HELP

The needs of family members whose loved one is receiving treatment for OCD are quite different from those of family members of someone who has received treatment and is learning the importance of relapse prevention. Your family member may not yet be diagnosed; perhaps you suspect he or she has OCD and you're in the process of collecting information. Throughout the book, we will strive to meet you where you are, providing information for all of these stages: prediagnosis, diagnosis, treatment, and maintenance. This book is not intended as a substitute for family therapy or psychological treatment by a qualified mental-health professional. Rather, it should be used in the following ways:

1. To help family members and friends learn how they can best support their loved one who is working though the process of breaking free from OCD, either with the help of a mental-health professional or through a self-help program, such as the one presented in *The OCD Workbook: Your Guide to Breaking Free from Obsessive-Compulsive Disorder* (Hyman and Pedrick 1999). You'll learn how to best support your loved one's recovery.

2. To assist people whose family member is reluctant to seek professional help for one reason or another. Educating yourself and making significant changes in how you respond to OCD symptoms may encourage a family member to seek help.

3. As a source of information for mental-health professionals who seek a better understanding of the effects of OCD on families and friends of people with OCD. This book can assist you as you provide support for these families.

This book will help you understand OCD, how it is diagnosed, its symptoms, the most effective treatments, and how family members are affected by OCD. It will help you develop a plan of action that can help each family member make positive changes to loosen the grip of OCD on your family. You will also learn the importance of caring for yourself and dealing effectively with stress.

Specific directions for applying the principles in this book are provided for spouses, friends, parents, and adult children of parents with OCD. Obsessive-compulsive disorder is often complicated by other illnesses such as depression, alcohol and drug addiction, trichotillomania, and body dysmorphic disorder. This book will discuss these and problems other family members may have, including OCD of their own. You'll learn how to find appropriate treatment for OCD and how to assess the treatment your loved one is receiving. This book will also give coping strategies for families whose loved ones are refusing treatment.

ABOUT THE AUTHORS

Karen J. Landsman, Ph.D., Clinical Psychologist

I am a licensed clinical psychologist specializing in the treatment of anxiety disorders in adults, children, teenagers, and families. Much of my practice is devoted to helping those with OCD and related disorders through the use of cognitive behavioral treatment methods. I present seminars at national and state psychological conferences, as well as write for national and local publications on matters of anxiety, OCD, and related disorders. I am also a member of the Scientific Advisory Board for the New Jersey Obsessive-Compulsive Foundation.

Helping families support a loved one with OCD is an important and rewarding part of my practice. In addition to taking a toll on the person with OCD, families are also substantially impacted by OCD. Reaching for outside help can be difficult for families, but without it, loved ones are not sure how to provide helpful support and are often left feeling discouraged. When people with OCD and their families confront the fears and obsessions of OCD, positive changes are always soon to follow. I am confident that sharing with you through this book will contribute to the health and well-being of your family.

Kathleen M. Rupertus, MA, MS

I am a psychotherapist who has specialized in the treatment of anxiety disorders since 1995. I work with children, adolescents, adults, and their family members at the Anxiety and Agoraphobia Treatment Center in Bala Cynwyd, Pennsylvania. My true passion is working with people who have OCD because I have had my own personal experience with OCD. As surprising as it may sound, I am truly thankful that OCD has been a part of my life. Even if I was somehow given the chance to have lived life *without* OCD, I wouldn't choose it. My painful struggle and eventual triumph over OCD has helped prepare me for where I am now in both my personal and professional life. I have learned and can teach others that there is joy and peace beyond the darkness of OCD.

Your loved one with OCD is fortunate that you have committed yourself to becoming a part of the recovery process. After reading this book and completing the exercises, you and your loved will be in the position to fight OCD through cooperation, dedication, and the use of proven behavioral strategies. Together, you and your loved one will become a powerful team. With that approach, OCD doesn't stand a chance.

Cherry Pedrick, RN

After twenty years working as a registered nurse, I made a career change. In 1995, I was diagnosed with OCD and applied cognitive behavioral therapy principles to break free. Writing helps me continue my progress keeping OCD at bay. I wrote several articles, then coauthored *The OCD Workbook* with Bruce Hyman, Ph.D., in 1999. Dr. Hyman and I teamed up again to write *Obsessive-Compulsive Disorder* and *Anxiety Disorders*, books to help teens understand OCD and other anxiety disorders. I also coauthored *The Habit Change Workbook* and *The BDD Workbook* with James Claiborn, Ph.D., and *Helping Your Child with OCD* with Lee Fitzgibbons, Ph.D.

Over the years, I've met many families struggling with OCD. My husband Jim and son James have been very supportive of me as I've dealt with OCD. I've witnessed the toll of OCD on their lives and recognize the great need family members like them have for support, knowledge, and a plan of action for meeting the challenge of living with OCD. I'm pleased to have the opportunity to assist Dr. Karen Landsman and Kathy Rupertus as they draw on their many years of experience with families struggling with OCD.

Chapter 1

OCD Defined

Do you feel like your home has been invaded? If you're living with someone with obsessive-compulsive disorder, in a way, it has been. You've been confronted by OCD, and your family needs to face the challenge as allies against a common opponent. OCD can be a brutal tyrant, demanding steadily increasing hours, money, and anguish. The goals of this book are to help you discover and confront how OCD is affecting you, to help you examine your relationship with the person with OCD and your family life, and to help you take positive steps toward a healthier, more constructive relationship with the person with OCD. This book will help you break free from the tyranny of OCD in your family.

You may be new to psychiatric illness and OCD, or perhaps it's been an ongoing struggle. Your loved one may be denying he or she even has OCD or may be finished with a course of treatment and struggling to prevent relapse. Wherever you are, the first step toward breaking free from the hold OCD has on your family is education. You need to know your opponent, OCD. This chapter will provide you with basic information about OCD: its definition, cause, and symptoms. Chapter 2 will give you a brief overview of the treatment of OCD.

We urge you to learn more about OCD and its treatment so you will know what your loved one is going through. *The OCD Workbook: Your Key to Breaking Free from Obsessive-Compulsive Disorder* (Hyman and Pedrick 1999) is an excellent place to start your pursuit of knowledge. There are a great many other excellent resources, and we've listed many in the resources section. With education, you'll be more equipped to provide support, help evaluate treatment options, and examine your response to OCD.

Knowledge of OCD and improved communication with your loved one will help you put the problems you're facing in perspective. With increasing knowledge and greater perspective, you'll be ready to make some important changes. Education and communication will provide a new perspective for understanding OCD symptoms and the ill-fated strategies family members have been using to deal with the symptoms. As you discover how OCD affects your family, you'll learn to change the way you respond to OCD symptoms. Healthier responses will help you break free from the effects of OCD. As you'll see, most of your changes will also make an impact on how your loved one handles OCD symptoms. Your gradual withdrawal from participating in rituals and avoidance, for example, will mean big changes in his or her response to obsessions.

WHAT IS OCD?

Obsessive-compulsive disorder is a neurobiobehavioral disorder characterized by obsessions and/or compulsions that are distressful, time-consuming, or interfere with routine daily functioning or relationships with others. Saying a disease is a *neurobiobehavioral disorder* means that it involves both dysregulation of the chemistry and circuitry of the brain and dysfunctional, learned patterns of thought and behavior. Mental-health professionals rely on the *Diagnostic and Statistical Manual of Mental Disorders (DSM-IV-TR)* to diagnose psychiatric illnesses. It states the following: "The essential features of Obsessive-Compulsive Disorder are recurrent obsessions or compulsions that are severe enough to be time consuming (i.e., they take more than one hour a day) or cause marked distress or significant impairment. At some point during the course of the disorder, the person has recognized that the obsessions or compulsions are excessive or unreasonable" (American Psychiatric Association [APA] 2000, 456-457).

Obsessions are persistent thoughts, impulses, ideas, or images that intrude into a person's thinking and cause excessive worry, anxiety, and distress. The thoughts are not what the person would expect or want to have, and he or she feels little control over them. Even so, the person does understand that the thoughts are a product of his or her own mind and are not imposed by others.

Compulsions are repetitive behaviors or mental acts that are performed in response to obsessions in order to relieve or prevent worry, anxiety, and distress. There may also be a vague goal of preventing or avoiding a dreaded event such as death, illness, or harm coming to self or others. Often the compulsions are unconnected to what they are meant to prevent. For example, turning a light switch on and off a lucky number of times may serve to keep a loved one safe from harm. This form of OCD is referred to as "magical thinking." When compulsions are logically connected to the feared outcome, such as hand washing to remove germs, they are clearly excessive. Repetitive mental acts can include counting, repeating words silently, praying, or going over events. Repetitive behaviors can include any type of behavior and are often called *rituals*. An important distinction between OCD and addictions is this: no gratification or pleasure is derived from compulsions. People with OCD get anxiety relief but no enjoyment from their compulsions.

Types of OCD

The obsessions and compulsions of OCD come in a variety of forms. Here, they are divided according to the type of compulsion. While some people have just one type of compulsion, many have symptoms from two or more categories. Often, you can also see a theme running through the obsessions. One person could have a general fear of harm or contamination coming to him- or herself, while another could have a fear of causing harm to others by doing something or neglecting to do something.

Checking

People with checking compulsions have irrational fears of harm coming to themselves or others if they don't engage in certain behaviors. They check such things as door locks, household appliances, stereo equipment, homework, and bills. Some people check on the health or well-being of others. Checking relieves the anxiety and distress of obsessive thoughts—at first. But the obsessive thoughts and worries soon return, and the person feels a need to check again. Over time, continued checking calls for more and more checking, accompanied by less relief.

Obsessive fears are usually related to the items checked, such as checking a light switch to make certain a light is off or turning a doorknob to make certain a door is locked. Sometimes, however, the fears and items checked are totally unrelated and have a magical quality, as in magical thinking. A person might have a fear that if electrical wires are touching, a loved one will get sick.

Washing and Cleaning

People with washing and cleaning compulsions engage in cleaning rituals in response to obsessions about contamination by germs, viruses, dirt, bodily fluids, chemicals, or other foreign substances. They relieve the distress caused by obsessive thoughts by washing their hands, showering, or cleaning things around them. They often demand that other family members participate in laundry or cleaning rituals. Over time, washing and cleaning brings less relief of anxiety, and rituals increase.

Ordering and Repeating

Some people with OCD relieve anxious thoughts by arranging certain items in particular ways. They may get upset if their personal belongings are rearranged and even insist that furniture in the house be arranged in a certain way. Over time, the demands for order continue to increase. There may also be a compulsion for symmetry or for the need to have certain things even. What if things are not in order or even? The result might be a vague feeling of uneasiness. It may include an aspect of magical thinking, such as fear of harm coming to a loved one or some disaster occurring. Others repeat routine activities over and over until they "feel right" or complete. They may do certain activities a particular number of times or count items such as books on a shelf or ceiling tiles. Such activities can be done in an effort to ward off unwanted intrusive thoughts or prevent harm.

Pure Obsessions

People with "pure obsessions" have thoughts or images of causing harm or danger to others. These are unwanted and intrusive thoughts that the person would not expect to have and are often frightening. The images might involve violent or sexual acts that are totally out of character for the person. It used to be thought that so-called pure obsessionals had only obsessions, but research into the nature of OCD reveals that most also have compulsions; it just takes a bit more digging to find them (Salkovskis 1985). Pure obsessionals have mental compulsions, which can take the form of counting, repeating certain words, or praying. They might also repetitively recall and review distressing situations in their minds, perhaps to reassure themselves that they did something "just right" or didn't make some catastrophic mistake. These mental compulsions are done to relieve the anxiety and distress caused by intrusive thoughts or to get rid of intrusive thoughts. At first, the person is rewarded with a temporary feeling of control and a lessening of anxiety, but soon the intrusive thoughts return and more compulsions are needed. The distressing result is that every waking hour becomes taken up by a cycle of obsessive thoughts counteracted by more and more compulsive thoughts and/or actions.

Hoarding

People with hoarding compulsions can amass large collections of useless things. While some of the items hold a sentimental value, many things they collect or fail to throw away are what others might consider trash or junk. This goes beyond the normal collecting of trinkets, souvenirs, rocks, movie tickets, baseball cards, and toys of childhood. For these people, letting go of collected items causes great distress, not just a few tears. Obsessive worries and emotions may relate to guilt over waste, pollution, or missed opportunities for recycling. Sometimes, people with hoarding OCD can explain the reason for the collections, but often they can't. In some ways, the collections almost become an extention of the person. Imagine the anxiety of having to get rid of a part of yourself, not just an item out of a collection.

Scrupulosity

Scrupulosity is a form of OCD with a religious, moral, or ethical theme. Obsessions can involve an excessive preoccupation with the possibility of having offended God or having violated the moral precepts of God in both thought and deed. Anxiety over the possibility of having committed sin leads to excessive prayer or repeated and unwarranted requests for grace and forgiveness from religious authorities, such as ministers, priests, and rabbis. Repeated requests for forgiveness are sought for even the most minute infractions. The person's participation in religious activities tends to go beyond the most devout of his or her faith. Instead of deriving peace and contentment from religious activities, the person seems to be seeking relief from distress from the constant worry that he or she may be committing a sin or offending God.

Everyday Compulsive Behaviors vs. OCD Compulsions

Most of us have a few obsessive thoughts and compulsive behaviors. Not everyone who checks the door twice before leaving the house has OCD. To better recognize the difference between people who check things meticulously and people with OCD, or between people who are very orderly and people with OCD, look back at the description of OCD in the *DSM-IV-TR* (APA 2000). The obsessions and compulsions must be time-consuming, cause marked distress or significant impairment, and be excessive or unreasonable.

The checking, washing, cleaning, and ordering of everyday life make life more organized and satisfying. In OCD, these behaviors interfere with life and cause distress. Compare the compulsive behaviors of your everyday life with OCD compulsions by completing the Compulsive Behaviors chart.

Compulsive Behaviors

List three behaviors you engage in regularly, almost ritualistically. Examples are exercising daily, organizing your sock drawer, and always eating dinner at a set time.

1. _____

2. _____

3. _____

Do these activities	Yes	No
Make your life more organized?	☐	☐
Give you pleasure?	☐	☐
Benefit others?	☐	☐
Take so much time that they interfere with your life?	☐	☐
Cause marked distress or significant impairment?	☐	☐
Seem excessive or unreasonable?	☐	☐

You may have checked no to the first three, and you probably checked no to the last three. These routine behaviors of everyday life may not always make life more organized, give pleasure, or benefit others, but they don't *greatly* interfere with your life or cause *marked* distress.

Describe how you feel if you can't engage in the behaviors you listed. Compare this to how your loved one appears to feel when he or she is unable to engage in an OCD ritual.

_____

_____

_____

_____

_____

Some people with OCD will have just one type of OCD symptom, checking things over and over to prevent harm, for example. Most people with OCD, however, don't fit into neat categories like the ones we described above. They may have two or more types of symptoms, with perhaps one being predominant and more disabling. One group of symptoms might subside and another might worsen over time. There is no consistent course of obsessive-compulsive disorder from person to person. It may masquerade as everyday behaviors, necessary worries, and commonsense cleanliness.

OTHER BEHAVIORS THAT LOOK LIKE OCD

Again, not every behavior that looks like OCD is OCD. Remember the criteria: the compulsions of OCD are time-consuming, cause marked distress or significant impairment, and are excessive or unreasonable. Even with these criteria, some behaviors fit better into another category.

Superstitions, Rituals, and Prayer

The *DSM-IV-TR* (APA 2000) points out that superstitions can be a normal part of life. They are indicative of OCD only when they are particularly time-consuming or result in significant impairment or distress. The *DSM-IV-TR* also specifies that ritualistic behavior must exceed cultural norms to be indicative of OCD. It needs to appear inappropriate to others of the same culture or religion who would be in the same type of circumstances. Examples would be religious practices such as prayer and worship.

Rituals are a common part of the day for most three-year-olds. They learn by repeating, and rituals give them confidence to deal with the outside world. As children become more comfortable with their surroundings, they let go of their rituals and give new behaviors a try. Lingering rituals tend to be related to bedtime, stressful situations, and times when children must separate from their parents. These usually disappear by age eight. Older children often continue to engage in a few rituals because they are fun and aid in learning. Many insist on wearing favorite clothes, especially for important events, and most children collect things. A classic example of a childhood ritual is the game of avoiding cracks in the sidewalk while chanting, "Step on a crack, break your mother's back!"

Adolescents and adults even keep rituals and superstitions as part of their repertoire of behaviors, without having OCD. Athletes engage in all kinds of rituals. Baseball players often kick the ground, touch their caps, spit, and perform many other actions when they go up to bat. Tennis players might bounce the ball with their rackets a certain number of times. Actors and public speakers, too, sometimes perform rituals to bring them luck or make them feel more comfortable.

How do these superstitious behaviors differ from the compulsive behaviors of OCD? The difference is the effect of the rituals on the person's life. When most children avoid cracks in the sidewalk, then accidentally step on one, it's no big deal. It's part of the game. There might be a slight momentary thought that something bad will happen, but it's easily dismissed. A young or especially sensitive child might have some uneasiness for a while until arriving home and finding Mom is okay. For the person with OCD, however, the mere idea of stepping on the crack may trigger intense anxiety and distress. Typically, another ritual would be needed to "undo" the possibility of future harm or danger.

Sports players, actors, and speakers can usually stop their rituals without too much difficulty if they wish. The behaviors don't interfere with their lives and they might feel like they enhance their lives, instead of disrupting them. Many people wear favorite outfits as soon as they're laundered. Others also feel compelled to collect certain items and feel they "just have to" complete the collection. The rituals of OCD are similar, but greatly exaggerated, with disruption of the rituals causing great distress. While adding to a treasured collection adds satisfaction and excitement to the lives of many, people with OCD experience no true pleasure or satisfaction while completing their rituals. Rather, they feel out of control—driven to perform the senseless rituals only as a means of reducing the severe distress and discomfort they're feeling.

Worry

Some people just seem to worry more than most. They worry about every detail of life. If this is greatly interfering with life, it can be a symptom of major depressive illness or an anxiety disorder called generalized anxiety disorder, or GAD. The worries of OCD are usually senseless or irrational but typically restricted to a specific theme, such as preventing harm or danger to others, and have compulsive behaviors associated with them.

Nervous Habits

What's the difference between the compulsions of OCD and nervous habits, such as thumb sucking or drumming fingers on a table? Habits are more automatic than compulsions. People tend to just find themselves doing them rather than engaging in them in response to an intrusive, disturbing thought. Compulsions and habits are both done to relieve anxiety, but with habits there is a general low-grade feeling of anxiety, while with OCD the compulsions are done to relieve the specific anxiety of an intrusive thought. Habits bring some degree of pleasure or satisfaction, at least in the beginning. Compulsions bring no pleasure, only anxiety relief. The difference can be subtle, and to complicate the issue even more, people with OCD may be a bit more prone to nervous habits.

Addictions and Pathological Gambling

The almost irresistible urges and desires to engage in certain activities are much like the obsessions of OCD. On the surface the behaviors associated with addictions and pathological gambling resemble the compulsions of OCD. But there's an important difference in that these behaviors are pleasure seeking. When chemicals or gambling are involved, the person craves and compulsively seeks a feeling of intoxication or high. In OCD, the goal of the compulsive behavior starts and ends with avoidance of distress and the attainment of a momentary sense of relief and control over that distress.

Eating Disorders

People with eating disorders such as anorexia nervosa, bulimia, and compulsive eating suffer from a preoccupation with food and thinness. Many have enough obsessive-compulsive symptoms to be diagnosed with OCD and can benefit from the same treatment strategies used for treating OCD.

Obsessive-Compulsive Personality Disorder

A *personality* is a consistent, enduring set of learned and inherited responses to situations and challenges of life. It is a set of characteristics or traits that don't change much over the life span. When personality traits consistently cause extreme difficulty in home and work life, a person may have a *personality disorder*. The *DSM-IV-TR* (APA 2000) describes a person with obsessive-compulsive personality disorder (OCPD) as someone with a preoccupation with details, rules, lists, orderliness, perfectionism, and mental and interpersonal control, at the expense of flexibility, openness, and efficiency. Such people tend to be highly predictable, to be overly routinized, to spurn change, and to keep their emotions under tight control.

These behavioral patterns are apparent in early adulthood and affect most areas of a person's life. People with OCD, on the other hand, may or may not have obsessive-compulsive personality traits. They may be excessively preoccupied with contamination with dirt and germs and take two-hour showers, but not at all concerned with orderliness or paying attention to details, for example. The biggest difference between OCD and OCPD is the degree of subjective distress. People with OCD are greatly distressed by their daily cycles of obsessive thoughts and compulsive behaviors, while those with OCPD tend not to be bothered by their overbearing, inflexible approach to life. As a result, people with OCPD often find themselves in frequent conflict with others in their work and personal lives.

WHAT CAUSES OCD?

Considerable research into the cause of OCD has focused upon the brain structures, circuitry, and neurochemical factors that may differentiate people with OCD from people without OCD. The brain structures in question include the basal ganglia, the orbital frontal cortex, and the cingulate gyrus. The basal ganglia is located in the center of the brain and includes the putamen, caudate nucleus, and amygdala. This is where information coming in from the outside world is sorted and unnecessary information is disregarded. These areas are also involved in controlling impulsiveness and reactions to fear. People with OCD become overwhelmed when intrusive thoughts are not disregarded.

The orbital cortex is located in the front of the brain, above the eyes. This is where we interpret the information coming in from the senses of sight, hearing, and touch. Emotions and moral judgments are applied to the information. Brain images of people with OCD show increased activity here. This area seems to keep people with OCD on alert, causing doubt, unease, and a need to be extra careful.

The cingulate gyrus is located in the center of the brain. This area alerts us to danger that something must be done to prevent disaster. It also helps with shifting from one thought or behavior to another. It's easy to see how a problem here could make a person with OCD get stuck on an obsessive thought or doing a ritual over and over.

Dr. Jeffrey Schwartz and Dr. Lewis Baxter demonstrated through positron-emission tomography (PET) scan studies that there was increased energy use in the orbital cortex in people with OCD (Schwartz and Beyette 1996). The exciting part about this research is that, after treatment with either medication or cognitive behavioral therapy, the overactivity in these areas of the brain decreased. Of course, there is a great deal more to learn, but this is an exciting reminder to people with OCD that "it's not you, it's OCD." It's a brain problem, and it can be helped.

A neurochemical imbalance also appears to be involved in OCD. *Serotonin* is an important neurotransmitter, a chemical messenger that enables communication between nerve cells. It plays a role in controlling many biological processes, including mood, aggression, impulses, sleep, appetite, body temperature, and pain. Medications that increase the amount of serotonin available to nerve cells in the brain improve obsessive-compulsive symptoms in people with OCD. Serotonin imbalance has also been implicated in depression, eating disorders, self-mutilation, and schizophrenia (Yaryura-Tobias and Neziroglu 1997).

Some cases of OCD (pediatric autoimmune neuropsychiatric disorder associated with streptococcal infections, or PANDAS) in children are associated with streptococcal infections. Other autoimmune diseases, such as Sydenham's chorea, rheumatic fever, and lupus, can also cause OCD. Studies have demonstrated a relationship with hypothalamic lesions, head trauma, and brain tumors. These are rare, however, as most cases of OCD occur without a specific, identifiable preceding traumatic event (Jenike 1998).

Research is being done to unlock the genetic basis of OCD. It appears that differences in specific genes or possibly several combinations of genes predispose a person to OCD. Studies done since 1930 have found OCD traits in the blood relatives of 20 to 40 percent of studied cases (Yaryura-Tobias and Neziroglu 1997). There appears to be even more of a genetic link in childhood-onset OCD (Geller 1998). Adding to this evidence are the findings of higher rates of OCD, Tourette's syndrome, and tics in relatives with OCD (Alsobrook and Pauls 1998).

Neurobiological differences make people with OCD more vulnerable to obsessive thoughts. Numerous studies have shown that almost all people at times have intrusive, unwanted, and unacceptable thoughts. The intrusive thoughts of people without OCD are basically no different from those of people with OCD.

The difference is the significance and importance assigned to the thoughts. Most people can experience their distressing thoughts, objectively evaluate them, and dismiss them almost immediately. For people with OCD, however, just having the thought gives it excessive importance, force, and meaning. It's as if the very act of thinking something bad will happen can somehow magically make it happen. They also tend to take excessive personal responsibility for prevention of harm associated with the thoughts. This combination of responses makes intrusive thoughts difficult to dismiss. It also heightens the anxiety and distress associated with the thoughts. The effort to suppress unacceptable thoughts has the boomerang effect of making them even stronger. As a result, even meaningless intrusive thoughts can be quite bothersome and cause distress because of their persistence and the feeling that they can't be controlled. We've all heard a tune replaying in our head over and over. Imagine hearing it louder and longer and feeling like it will never, ever end.

The anxiety and efforts to suppress the intrusive, obsessive thoughts begin a cycle of obsessions and compulsions that is extremely difficult to break. The cycle perpetuates itself as compulsions assure the occurrence of future obsessions and compulsions. People with OCD engage in compulsions to get rid of the anxiety and distress caused by obsessive thoughts. These behaviors or thoughts are meant to prevent disaster, avoid blame or responsibility, make things right, or make the thoughts go away. Most people with OCD know, at least to some degree, that their rituals don't do what they're meant to do. Knowing this causes even more distress, anxiety, shame, and embarrassment.

Over time, compulsions may lose their ability to bring about relief of anxiety. Checking and washing may not bring about the same level of relief, so often more and more checking and washing must be done. Showers become longer and must be done according to rigidly applied rules. More objects need to be checked before leaving the house in an attempt to obtain relief from obsessive thoughts. If an intrusive thought occurs while passing through a doorway, a person might then decide to tap both sides of the door three times instead of just tapping one side twice. Compulsions can grow more elaborate, time-consuming, and complex. Obsessions and compulsions have many ways of changing, evolving, and multiplying. In the process of checking to relieve one obsession, another potential threat can be brought to a person's attention. One more thing then needs to be checked. Obsessive worry and contemplation can also add to the list of compulsions. If hands need to be washed in one circumstance and in another circumstance could be just as dangerous, then it stands to reason that hands need to be washed then too. One set of fears sometimes seems to subside only to be replaced by another set of worries and fears. As time passes, and for no apparent reason, checking may lose its importance and give way to contamination fears and cleaning rituals.

Again, most people with OCD know deep down that their worries and fears are senseless, at least some of the time. But in the midst of an OCD episode, the doubt intensifies and the worries feel very real and necessary. The need to check, wash, or put things in order feels overwhelmingly crucial. The need for absolute certainty takes over. Not only do compulsions fail to effectively relieve anxiety and distress caused by obsessions, but they also heap on greater anxiety. Engaging in compulsions brings about the added anxiety for people with OCD of knowing they're engaging in unnecessary, time-consuming, irrational, senseless, and embarrassing behaviors.

Doubt and uncertainty feed obsessive thoughts and keep a person actively engaged in doing compulsions. Often, compulsions take the form of persistent questions and pleas for reassurance from loved ones. These compulsions are sometimes hard to detect and are among the most difficult to gain control of.

OCD IN CHILDREN

About 2.5 percent of the population will develop OCD in their lifetime. Among children, the prevalence is .5 to 1 percent. Average onset is around 10.2 years old. The disorder tends to develop earlier in boys than in girls. About two-thirds of people with OCD have their first symptoms before age twenty-five, most often between age nine and thirteen (Niehous and Stein 1997). Nearly half of adults with OCD have an onset in childhood (March and Mulle 1998). Most didn't get help until much later, however. With today's improved understanding and knowledge of mental illness and the increasing availability of effective treatment, these statistics should improve.

In most children, the first appearance of obsessive-compulsive symptoms tends to be mild and doesn't interfere much with normal activities. For others, onset is sudden, almost overnight. In these cases, doctors may suspect PANDAS. However, often children will keep their obsessions and compulsions a secret. Parents may finally see their child's rituals when they become more overwhelming for the child and cannot be hidden. The onset of OCD often appears to occur suddenly when it has actually been a gradual process. Some people with OCD can look back and define a specific triggering event or set of events, such as the death of a loved one, divorce of parents, illness, or moving and changing schools. Most, however, can identify no specific trauma or challenging event when symptoms first occurred. Indeed, everyone at some time experiences distressing life circumstances, and most people don't develop OCD or other anxiety disorders. The cause appears to lie more within the brain itself than without. It seems that stressful events could trigger OCD symptoms but only in those vulnerable people who are already "wired" for OCD.

PANDAS

A subset of children with OCD have what is known as pediatric autoimmune neuropsychiatric disorders associated with streptococcal infections, or PANDAS. It starts with a group A beta-hemolytic streptococci (GABHS) infection, or strep throat. The strep infection is no worse than most. The problem is the body's reaction to the infection. The body produces antibodies to fight it. In children who are genetically predisposed to OCD and tics, these antibodies attack the basal ganglia area of the brain, producing OCD symptoms and/or tics. PANDAS occurs most often in children from three years old to puberty. The first episode usually occurs several months after an acute strep infection. Further episodes occur days or weeks after another infection.

Children with PANDAS experience a rapid onset of symptoms, followed by a period of complete remission. The patterns can recur several times. Other neurological symptoms may be present, such as tics, hyperactivity, handwriting changes, sensitivity to touch or clothing tags, irritability, mood changes, loss of math skills, fidgeting, impulsivity, poor attention span, and separation anxiety. In some instances *choreiform movements*, such as grimacing, clumsiness, trembling, or involuntary and irregular writhing movements of the legs, arms, or face, may also be evident. Treatment of PANDAS involves prompt detection and treatment of the strep infection, most often with the use of antibiotics. Symptoms improve with treatment but residual symptoms can remain. Subsequent strep infections can aggravate existing OCD symptoms

---

THE SECRET WORLD OF OCD

More than with other psychiatric disorders, people with OCD live with high levels of shame and embarrassment about their symptoms. The nature of OCD symptoms fosters a powerful tendency to keep the symptoms hidden from others, sometimes even from closest family members. Some people with OCD are successful in hiding all of their rituals. They live in a secret world of obsessive thoughts and compulsive behaviors. Most will reveal part of this world to those closest to them, but even then they often aren't willing to share many of their most embarrassing rituals.

A great deal of energy might go into keeping rituals secret. A woman who checks appliances in the kitchen before going to bed or leaving the house may not tell family members about fears that, in the process of checking the stove, she may have inadvertently turned the stove on, thus making it necessary to check it over and over. People who take hour-long showers are often reluctant to share the details of their showers, afraid others wouldn't understand why each body part must be washed in a particular order and for a certain length of time. When the family is let in on the secret obsessions and compulsions, the extent often isn't revealed. Checking something in another room might be disguised as forgetfulness as a person feigns going back for a forgotten item. Someone can disguise an obsessive thought about contamination by deliberately getting his or her hands dirty so they can be washed with a legitimate excuse.

Understanding OCD Helps the Family Break Free

Often, the family as a whole is involved in keeping the secrets. Family members may believe they can help the person overcome the compulsions, or at least contain them at home until the person can get them under control. At first, they might appear to be helping their loved one, but OCD symptoms progress over time. Eventually they consume more and more of a person's life and more and more of the family's life. Family members may attempt to rescue their loved one by giving in to demands for extra laundry loads, special soaps or cleaning supplies, or ridding the house of "dangerous" products. Unfortunately, such rescue behaviors only serve to feed OCD symptoms. As more and more time and energy is spent completing rituals, there is less time and energy to devote to other, more enjoyable activities. The result is increasing loneliness and isolation. As family members attempt to adjust to their loved one's OCD, they may also experience social withdrawal and isolation.

You can't change your response to your family member with OCD until you begin to understand the compelling internal forces that are behind such a confusing array of behaviors. A healthy perspective and an accepting atmosphere will show your family member that you recognize who the opponent is: the disease of OCD.

THE EXPERIENCE OF OCD

This book includes stories about several families living with OCD. Except for Cherry Pedrick and her family, these family portraits are composites of real families. They will help to illustrate important points throughout the book. You can meet the families now.

The Roberts Family

On the way to work one day, Deon Roberts was struck with the thought that he hadn't locked his front door. He turned his car around and went home to check the door. It was locked. He didn't think about that incident again until months later, when his worries about the front door became more frequent. He was late for work several times a week because he kept going back to check the door. He also worried about the stove and other appliances, his computer, the lights, and his electric shaver. What if they were left on? Perhaps they could start a fire. One day, out of exasperation, Deon's wife Alisha helped him check everything before he left the house. This relieved his fears. Now, if someone broke into the house or a fire started, he wouldn't be to blame. Alisha rearranged her work schedule so she could leave the house after Deon, promising to check everything before leaving. Deon's OCD was confusing for Alisha. He hadn't been like this when they'd married four years earlier. She hoped he could get better before they had children.

Leaving his office became just as big a chore. Deon checked his computer and radio to make sure they were off. Finally, one day he unplugged everything before leaving, sure that would satisfy his fears. Then he checked the plugs with his fingers to make sure they were indeed unplugged. Deon also had difficulty leaving his car. He put the brake on every time he parked, then often checked to make sure it was indeed secure. He worried that he hadn't locked the door and usually went back to check the door at least once after parking the car.

The Jacobs Family

When Marilyn and Harold Jacobs first married, her OCD was mild, but it became more severe with each pregnancy. For women who have a predisposition for OCD, it sometimes becomes apparent or worsens during pregnancy. With three young children, her OCD became overwhelming and her marriage strained. Marilyn was exhausted and had little time for her family because her days and most of her evenings were filled with housecleaning, laundry, and showering. She would scrub floors, walls, and kitchen utensils over and over in an endless, exhaustive effort to rid her family of any possible "contamination" from dirt or germs they may have carried in from the outside world.

Marilyn's fear was that unless she rid her home of all possible contamination, she'd be guilty of harming her children. When Harold, a computer technician, returned home from work each day, Marilyn insisted that he remove all of his clothing in the garage prior to entering the house, then wash his hands and feet with a solution of bleach and water, and finally take a shower while she "decontaminated" his clothing in the laundry. The daily routine, while annoying, became an accepted part of daily life for the family. Any attempt to resist the pattern or not complete it perfectly resulted in Marilyn having severe rages and panic symptoms. To keep the peace, her husband complied.

The Smith Family

Robert and Dorothy Smith were quite familiar with OCD. Robert had struggled with obsessive thoughts and urges to have everything even and in order since childhood. Cognitive behavioral therapy had helped, and he now had only mild symptoms. When their daughter Joan began to express obsessive thoughts and check her belongings over and over, they were quick to recognize her OCD symptoms. Joan sought reassurance from her parents that she hadn't caused harm by doing something wrong, neglecting to do something, or not praying correctly.

After dropping out of high school, Joan lived at home and worked at several low-paying part-time jobs. She wasn't able to keep a job for very long because of her anxiety and checking. Her parents worried that she would never be independent. Robert's own experience with OCD made it difficult for him to become closely involved in helping Joan in ways she needed from him. For instance, he avoided situations that triggered his daughter's symptoms as a means of protecting her from OCD.

The Parks Family

At the age of twenty-five, Gene Parks wanted to settle down and raise a family, but he despaired that it would ever happen. He felt like he had nothing to offer someone else, and his life just seemed too complicated. Even with a college degree, he had difficulty keeping a job. Employers were initially impressed with his attention to details but soon became exasperated with his slowness, difficulty making decisions, and insistence on checking his work. He'd get more nervous as the pressure mounted, and soon he'd be looking for work again. At home, Gene spent many hours needlessly checking appliances and electrical cords to make certain they were safe, bills and paperwork for accuracy, and doors and windows at night to make certain they were locked. He called his brother Stan frequently to ask for help making simple decisions.

The Gonzalez Family

It's not hard to find things to fear in today's world. José Gonzalez's wife Rita found it increasingly difficult to reassure him that his fears were unfounded. Spooked by local news stories of the dangers of common household chemicals and sprays, he insisted on removing all chemicals from the house and garage, including insecticides, fertilizers, and even cleaning products. He warned his wife about the use of hair products, makeup, and vitamins. To him, these were all poisons that posed an immediate threat to his family's health. With further news reports of severe acute respiratory syndrome (SARS) and anthrax, he became afraid to leave the house.

When José wasn't scouring the Internet for information on the harmful effects of chemicals and cleaning products, he was placing things in order. He insisted on everything being in exactly the right place. José was a college student, and he was late for class several days each week due to his repeatedly checking the order of things in his backpack.

The Delaney Family

Cleaning, hand washing, and showering rituals had been a part of Mario Delaney's life for most of his life. As he grew up, his OCD rituals had become a part of his family's life as well. He was thirty-five years old and still lived with his parents, Louis and Rose. He worked for the family business, mostly doing paperwork. Although Mario was capable of much more, this job protected him from interacting with customers and thus coming into contact with other triggers to his contamination fears and hand washing. He kept to himself, seeing no reason for going out much or relating with people other than his family. His rituals kept him busy enough, and the thought of trying to maintain his OCD secret from those outside the family was just too much for Mario to consider.

Mario was not alone in his world of OCD. Over the years, his family members had inadvertently become a part of the OCD cycle through their frequent accommodations and reassurances. Finally, at the urging of his parents, brothers, and sisters, Mario decided to try once more to make some changes. He had lost enough to OCD, and he wanted more from his life than his OCD would allow. His family supported his efforts as he progressed in his therapy, and it was Mario who approached his family about their accommodating behaviors and the need to develop new ways of responding to his OCD. As his family members developed a new understanding of OCD, they were able to become more supportive and intervene therapeutically when confronted with OCD moments.

The Chandler Family

It took years for Sandy Chandler to amass her vast collection of magazines, books, and newspapers. They were stacked from floor to ceiling in all the rooms of her home with paths like a maze throughout. She said she could find each book and periodical on a moment's notice. Sandy also collected cats. When their number approached one hundred and she couldn't care properly for them, the neighbors complained about the odor and the cats roaming in their yards. Sandy's family tried to convince her to find homes for some of the cats, get the rest neutered, and get help for her hoarding, but to no avail. Eventually, animal control intervened.

The Lyons Family

Melinda Lyons's OCD was much more severe than the OCD experienced by the other people you've met here. At the age of fifty, she lived at home with her elderly parents. They were very involved in helping her perform her many rituals. She engaged in elaborate counting rituals before doing almost any activity. To get her to eat, her parents participated in the rituals. She would eat very few foods and only those purchased at a particular store. The family bought special cleaning products so she could decontaminate her room and bathroom. Melinda's parents worried about what would happen to her when they died or were too old to care for her needs.

The Peters Family

Linda Peters took hour-long showers every morning and when she returned home from school or other activities. She also showered before going to bed. The idea of moving two hundred miles away to college and living in a dorm room with a roommate was what finally galvanized Linda to tackle her OCD. Her parents, John and Melody, had been concerned about Linda's frequent hand washing and showering, and had tried to get her to make changes. Up until now, Linda hadn't shown much interest in tackling her OCD, but now she was motivated by her desire to gain her independence and attend college. Both Linda and her parents were determined to make recovery a family priority.

Cherry Pedrick and Her Family

In 1999, Cherry Pedrick coauthored *The OCD Workbook* with Dr. Bruce Hyman. She is recovering from OCD and continues that lifelong recovering process. It may be surprising that she still considers herself to be "recovering" or that her family still considers her to be recovering, but that is an important concept. Vigilance is an important part of breaking free from the tyranny of OCD and not letting it take over again. The OCD usually continues to lurk in the corners of a person's mind, waiting to pounce if given a chance. Cherry still feels the urge to check and make certain she's done things correctly or ask for reassurance that she's not done harm to another. Her husband and son still have to deal with occasional unwarranted questions. This book shares some of the ways her family has dealt with OCD. They're healthy, happy, and whole. This chapter ends with a poem Cherry wrote when she was first diagnosed with OCD. It expresses her feelings toward all who have supported her efforts toward recovery.

I'm Not Crazy
By Cherry Pedrick

I'm not crazy, not really.
I know I act strange at times.
I know I ask too many questions.
I know the door was locked, and you watched me turn the car around
. . . again . . . to check the lock . . . again.
But I'm not crazy.

Her hands are red and raw.
She hides them in her lap or behind her back.
But still, she wonders if they're really clean.
"I did touch the doorknob, not with my hands, of course, with my sleeve.
But now I've touched my sleeve."

She needs to wash her hands again.
But she's not crazy.
"Don't come in. Well, okay, come in.
But don't look around. Don't judge my house."
He knows he has boxes of paper, magazines,
And newspapers cluttering the rooms.
But he knows where his taxes from 1962 are
... and the utility bills ... and the canceled checks.
But he's not crazy.

She walked through the door, but she didn't do it right.
She knows it was the eighth time.
"One more time, I've got to get it right."
If she doesn't do it right, something may happen to her mother.
But she's not crazy.

My mind wanders when you're talking to me.
When you look at me strangely,
I pull my thoughts together and try to concentrate on your words.
But I can't quite give you my full attention.
My mind is filled with worries and fears I can't seem to release.
But I'm not crazy.

We're not crazy, not really.
We know these behaviors and thoughts aren't normal,
That they're irrational.
But we do them anyway.
Do "crazy" people know they're acting irrational?
No, they act and think with ignorance of their strangeness.
They don't see your stares or hear your whispers.
They don't hear the other children laugh.
They don't see their families' worried faces.
Oh, the bliss of not knowing, of not caring,
Of not longing to stop checking, washing, hoarding,
Ritualizing, and worrying.

But of course, we do want to stop,
We do want to be "normal" like you.
We dream of a day without these tortured thoughts.
I will leave my house without worrying about the lock.
And she won't have to go through a door more than once.
His house will be clean and her hands will be healed.
My mind won't be filled with worries and fears.

It's not a dream.
With therapy, medication, prayer, and putting my life in God's hands,

My dream has come true. Well, almost.
I have a few strange behaviors and I still worry at times.
But doesn't everyone?

I remember the stares, the whispers, the worried faces, and the laughs.
Each day, the memories fade a little more.
But I remember so well, the kind support, the gentle encouragement,
And the firm insistence that I resist my temptation
To quit trying and give in to my compulsions.
I remember the times my loved ones laughed with me
When I was finally able to see the humor in my behavior and thoughts.
They rejoiced in my success, even my small steps toward success.
Most of all, I remember the love and prayers.
They prayed when I couldn't.
They loved me when I couldn't love myself.

I think I speak for many with this strange illness called OCD,
"Thank you who have supported me and others with OCD.
Without you, our recovery would be slower.
We might not see the need for recovery, we might lose hope."
To those who laugh and stare and whisper—to you I say, "I'm not crazy."

Summary

Obsessive-compulsive disorder is a neurobiobehavioral disorder. This means that it involves dysregulation of the chemistry and circuitry of the brain as well as a person's dysfunctional, learned patterns of thought and behavior. It is often characterized by shame because people struggling with the disorder know their behaviors are strange or embarrassing to loved ones. Knowledge about OCD is the first step toward recovery.

As someone who cares for someone with OCD, you may also feel embarrassment, even shame at times. You've probably felt helpless and frustrated. As you've seen, you and your family are not alone in your struggle with OCD. You've taken the first step toward understanding healthier ways to respond to OCD and support a person struggling with OCD. Part of your frustration and hopelessness is due to not knowing what to do. As you learn better support methods, many of these feelings will be replaced with hope for a new future for your family.

Chapter 2

Treatment of OCD

For decades, people with OCD suffered in secret. Even when they revealed their secrets, adequate treatment was unavailable. Today, thanks to advances in neuropsychiatric research, there is a greater understanding of OCD in the medical community and in the general population. People are emerging from the shadows and discovering that they have a very treatable disease. Millions of people with OCD are learning that they can break free from their obsessive-compulsive symptoms and live productive, satisfying lives.

Clinical research has repeatedly demonstrated that cognitive behavioral therapy (CBT) and medications called selective serotonin reuptake inhibitors are the most effective treatments for OCD. Both work well, but CBT has a major advantage over medication. It lasts! While medication generally stops working when it is discontinued, the beneficial effects of CBT continue even after therapy ends. When CBT is used, medication can also play an important role; it can ease the obsessions enough to allow a person to participate in CBT.

This chapter will briefly introduce you to medication therapy and CBT for OCD. Many books describe the cognitive behavioral therapy principles and the medications that are employed to treat obsessive-compulsive disorder. For further clarification, you can refer to one of the books listed under self-help in the resources section at the back of this book.

MEDICATION THERAPY

Medication can be an important part of OCD treatment. Remember that OCD is a neurobiobehavioral problem. Researchers have looked at the biological component and developed medications that are effective at weakening obsessive thoughts and the urges to perform rituals. Medications, however, rarely eliminate OCD symptoms entirely. Sometimes, people start medication thinking they won't need CBT. While medications often reduce the force and intensity of symptoms, the learned behavioral "habits" acquired from the OCD often remain unless modified using CBT principles. Medication therapy, while clearly effective at reducing OCD symptoms, should be considered only a partial answer to the question of how to manage OCD symptoms to live a normal, productive life.

On the other hand, cognitive behavioral therapy without medication is considered appropriate for many people who have mild to moderate OCD and are highly motivated. Medication combined with CBT is a common option when symptoms are severe or when a person is reluctant or fearful of participating in CBT. In this case, medication is often started first. Then, as symptoms ease somewhat, the person can have a much better response to CBT. In general, medication is considered in these instances:

- The OCD is moderate to severe.

- There is resistance to participating in CBT.

- Complicating conditions, such as severe depression or panic disorder, are present.

- Cognitive behavioral therapy seems just too hard.

- Cognitive behavioral therapy is not available in the area.

Antidepressants called serotonin reuptake inhibitors (SRIs) and selective serotonin reuptake inhibitors (SSRIs) are used for the treatment of OCD. In addition to reducing obsessive-compulsive symptoms, they have positive effects on depression and anxiety. Selective serotonin reuptake inhibitors work by making more serotonin available in the *synapses* (small spaces) that join nerve cells in the brain. This improves the transmission of impulses or messages from one cell to another in important areas of the brain. Clomipramine (Anafranil) is an older serotonin reuptake inhibitor and differs in that it also directly affects other vital neurotransmitters such as norepinephrine, which is important for some OCD patients.

Medications used to treat OCD include clomipramine (Anafranil), fluoxetine (Prozac), fluvoxamine (Luvox), paroxetine (Paxil), sertraline (Zoloft), citalopram (Celexa), venlafaxine (Effexor), and the newest one, escitalopram (Lexapro). It takes six to twelve weeks on a medication to see improvement of OCD symptoms. Every individual's body is different, and each SSRI works a bit differently, so two or more medications may need to be tried before finding the right one. It is important to give each medication an adequate trial period unless the prescribing psychiatrist decides that severe side effects contradict this. Sometimes none of the SSRIs seem to help alone, and additional medications are necessary.

What kind of results can be expected? Will the OCD suddenly disappear? Does the person with OCD wake up one morning feeling anxiety free, happy, and relieved of depression? Probably not. The effects are generally gradual. When Cherry first took medication for OCD and depression, she looked in the mirror one day and thought for sure her eyes had changed color. They looked brighter and greener. Well, of course, they hadn't changed color, but the lines of depression in her face had eased. Her eyes were smiling! For several weeks, the depression and anxiety had gradually improved. That day, looking at her "smiling eyes," Cherry felt hope that she would get better and felt empowered to fight the OCD. The obsessions were still there, but they were less intense. She still felt the compulsion to check things but felt more confident she could learn to resist it. Cherry was now open to learning about CBT and applying the strategies needed to fight back against the OCD.

Medication can decrease OCD symptoms and make them easier to fight with CBT. It can decrease depression and anxiety, motivating a person to get well and get on with life. For those for whom medication makes a difference, it is reasonable to stay on it indefinitely. For those who have not received CBT, the relapse rate from discontinuing medication is 80 to 90 percent (Yaryura-Tobias and Neziroglu 1997). However, for those patients needing to discontinue medication for one of various reasons, such as pregnancy, a course of CBT can enable them to manage symptoms better.

The choice to stay on medication is strictly a medical decision that each patient must consider with the counsel of his or her doctor. It has nothing to do with character. Therefore, people who make this choice should never be considered weak or lacking in toughness. For some, where the biological component is stronger, medication plays a more important role.

COGNITIVE BEHAVIORAL THERAPY

Cognitive behavioral therapy and medication have become the treatments of choice for OCD. Why CBT? Put simply, because it works. Other treatments have been tried, but research has proven CBT to be an effective treatment. Not just any CBT, however. Just because a treatment program is labeled CBT doesn't mean it's appropriate for OCD. Cognitive behavioral therapy is used to treat many problems, including anxiety, aggression, depression, attention-deficit/hyperactivity disorder, pain, and learning disabilities. Different cognitive behavioral techniques are used for each of these areas.

Cognitive behavioral therapy brings together two treatment approaches. *Behavior therapy* refers to strategies that help people change specific problem behaviors. The cornerstone of OCD treatment is behavior therapy that focuses on *exposure and ritual prevention* (also called *exposure and response prevention*, ERP or E/RP). It involves deliberate exposure to situations that cause fear, anxiety, and distress, and not engaging in the usual ritual. *Cognitive therapy* refers to strategies that help people examine and change distorted thinking and faulty beliefs. Emotions and behaviors are determined, in part, by how we interpret circumstances and situations. Cognitive techniques can help people evaluate situations and learn more positive ways of responding to them. Alone, cognitive techniques have not been shown to be very effective in the treatment of OCD, but cognitive and behavioral techniques complement each other. How we think affects how we behave, so changing our thinking patterns can encourage and support behavior change.

Cognitive behavioral therapy provides people with OCD with the tools needed to manage obsessive-compulsive symptoms. Instead of a time-limited treatment, it's best to look at it as a lifestyle change. Think of cognitive behavioral strategies as survival skills.

Exposure and Ritual Prevention

Exposure and ritual prevention involves voluntary exposure to situations that cause anxiety, fear, or distress. At first, the person with OCD is quite anxious, but thanks to a natural, built-in process, courtesy of our central nervous systems, called *habituation*, the anxiety diminishes on its own. With repeated, prolonged contact to a feared object or situation, the person's nervous system gets used to the situation, or habituates to it. The second part of ERP is *ritual prevention*. This means facing the feared situation and not engaging in the usual ritual as a means of reducing the anxiety. At first, the person with OCD might delay, shorten, or change the ritual, but the eventual goal is to eliminate the need for the ritual, thereby stopping it completely.

It might be hard to imagine your loved one stopping all rituals, and that isn't the immediate goal. A therapist first has the patient make a list of all his or her obsessions, compulsions, and situations avoided due to the OCD. Next, the patient develops a hierarchy of feared situations, listing them from least to most fear provoking. The patient tackles a situation that produces mild or moderate anxiety first, and then works on a situation further up on the list. Not all feared situations can be re-created, of course. Obsessive fears of getting sick or harming someone else, for example, can be handled with *imaginal exposure*. This involves prolonged, repeated visualization of a feared situation, perhaps by recording a scenario and listening to it over and over.

If your loved one is receiving appropriate treatment for his or her OCD, *exposure, ritual prevention,* and *cognitive behavioral therapy* are familiar terms. If these terms aren't familiar, and you and your loved one aren't certain the treatment he or she is receiving is the most effective, read chapter 11 now. We'll help you assess the treatment and find more appropriate treatment for OCD. What if your loved one is refusing treatment or even refusing to believe that he or she has OCD? In chapter 11, we also discuss coping strategies for living under the strain of untreated OCD. You'll learn how to apply much of the information in this book to these situations.

Cognitive Strategies

People with OCD get caught up in their fears and rituals. On one level, they know their rituals are unnecessary, but on another level, they believe they need to do them, "just in case." Often there is a danger to be avoided, however insignificant.

Cognitive strategies are aimed at confronting the distorted thoughts and beliefs that sustain the rituals. Alone, cognitive strategies have little effect on OCD symptoms. After all, people with OCD have often spent years trying to talk themselves out of performing their rituals. They've tried to convince themselves that their beliefs are untrue, even absurd. The power of cognitive therapy lies in its correct combination with exposure and ritual prevention.

Cognitive restructuring is a strategy that directly challenges thought patterns that encourage obsessive-compulsive behaviors. People with OCD possess strong beliefs about the likelihood of a given situation being dangerous to themselves or others. Often the belief is not supportable by the facts. This makes the belief a faulty one. Cognitive restructuring helps the person with OCD identify inaccurate beliefs and attitudes and replace them with accurate, healthier ones. Below are some typical faulty beliefs of people with OCD with examples of each from *The OCD Workbook* (Hyman and Pedrick 1999). Your loved one may be learning about these types of faulty beliefs during treatment.

Black/White, All-or-Nothing Thinking

"If I'm not perfectly safe, then I'm in great, overwhelming danger."

"If I don't do it perfectly, then I've done it horribly."

Magical Thinking

"If I think of a bad, horrible thought, it will certainly cause something bad or horrible to happen."

Overestimation of Risk and Harm

"A one-in-a-million chance of something bad happening is exactly the same as a 99.999 percent chance of something bad happening."

Perfectionism

"It is intolerable unless I do it perfectly."

Hypermorality

"I'll certainly go to hell [be punished severely] for even the slightest mistake, error, or miscue."

Overresponsibility for Others

"I must always, at all times, guard against making a mistake that can possibly, even remotely, harm an innocent person."

Thought/Action Fusion (Similar to Magical Thinking)

"If I have a bad, even horrible, thought about harming someone, it feels just like I've actually done it."

Overimportance of Thought

"My thoughts are an extremely important determinant of what I actually do."

The Exclusivity Error

"If something bad is going to happen, it is much more likely to happen to me or someone I love or care about than others."

The "Nobility Gambit" (Also Known As the Martyr Complex or Sacrificial Lamb)

"How noble and wonderful I am! I'll gladly suffer or sacrifice my life doing endless rituals [washing, counting, checking, etc.] all day long as a small price to pay to protect those I love from danger and harm. And since no one close to me has yet to die or suffer, I must be doing something right!"

"What If" Thinking

"In the future, what if I . . . do it wrong?"

> . . . make a mistake?"

> . . . get AIDS?"

> . . . am responsible for causing harm to someone?"

Intolerance of Uncertainty

"I can't relax until I'm 100 percent certain of everything and know that everything will be okay. If I'm uncertain about *anything* [my future, the health of myself or loved ones], it is intolerable."

Challenging Faulty Beliefs

After a person indentifies his or her faulty beliefs, the next step is to systematically challenge them. Rather than just telling themselves to "Stop thinking that way!" people with OCD learn to better observe their own thoughts. This helps them to more realistically appraise their thoughts and to discover faulty beliefs that feed their obsessions and compulsive behaviors. Often, they will be asked to write down unrealistic appraisals and faulty beliefs. This means identifying OCD-based thoughts and labeling them as such. They will then be asked to challenge these unrealistic appraisals with more realistic appraisals of situations, using actual facts.

Other cognitive exercises can help a person with OCD understand on a deeper level that his or her thoughts truly don't cause bad events to happen. The following exercise from *The OCD Workbook* illustrates how this works: "Choose an old small appliance (like a toaster) that is known to be in good working order. Every day for one week write on a piece of paper: 'The toaster will break.' Write it one hundred times and picture it in your mind each time. After one week, examine the outcome. Did your thoughts affect the operation of the toaster?" (Hyman and Pedrick 1999, 102). Of course, thinking about the toaster breaking would not affect its operation. In the same way, thinking about something bad happening won't cause it to happen, even though OCD thoughts tell your loved one they will. This type of cognitive exercise can chip away at the power of these faulty beliefs.

Cognitive strategies can be a powerful tool as your loved one challenges his or her overresponsibility for harm coming to others. The "pie technique" can help attribute responsibility for negative events more accurately and appropriately. The person with OCD might imagine a mishap or accident. Then, he or she imagines every possible factor that could contribute to such an accident. Each factor is written on a pie chart, showing its possible contribution to the imagined accident. This helps the person with OCD understand that even if feared things were to happen, he or she wouldn't be totally at fault. Even if something has already happened, it helps to give a more realistic assessment of the situation.

Summary

This chapter has given you a brief overview of a few cognitive strategies used in *The OCD Workbook*. There and in the many other resources listed in the back of this book, your loved one can find helpful exercises for combating faulty beliefs and unhealthy self-talk. People have a tendency to tell themselves some very negative things. Being more positive with the way you talk to yourself can reduce anxiety and depression and ease much of the tension in relationships. This isn't so-called positive thinking but realistic thinking.

Medication can be an important part of the treatment of OCD. It can decrease depression, anxiety, and OCD symptoms, assisting in the fight to wipe out OCD through cognitive behavioral therapy. Some people find it best to stay on a combination of medication and CBT indefinitely, while others will, with a doctor's assistance, choose to decrease or stop medication after completing CBT. Both treatments are good choices.

Chapter 3

The Inner Workings of OCD

You and your family will likely need to make long-term changes in the way you handle OCD symptoms. Family contracts can help you make more effective decisions as you respond to OCD behaviors. As a spouse or partner, parent, or other family member, choosing to respond and act differently can be difficult. In order to help yourself and your loved one, you both need to develop a better understanding of the "inner workings" of OCD. How did OCD become so demanding? How has it come to rule so powerfully over your loved one's life? How has it come to rule so powerfully over you and your family?

OCD: A NEUROBIOBEHAVIORAL DISORDER

OCD can be considered a neurobiobehavioral disorder because it is thought to be associated with neurological, biological, and behavioral dysfunction. The neurological aspects refer to the different structures or parts of the brain that appear to play a part in OCD. The biological aspects refer to the genetics and chemical functions within the brain that are associated with OCD. Together, abnormalities within the structures of the brain and abnormalities in the chemical functioning of the brain give rise to OCD symptoms and dysfunctional behaviors. We refer to the resulting dysfunctional behaviors as rituals, or *compulsions*. Rituals are often the most visible aspects of OCD—they are the parts of OCD that you can most easily observe. Rituals are the repeated checking, hand washing, touching, reassurance seeking, or other repetitive behaviors that cause so much pain and frustration.

The OCD Command Center

Now let's look at how the neurobiobehavioral aspects of OCD combine with aspects of "normal" brain functioning to create the vicious cycle that is OCD. Think of the "normal" brain as having a "worry part" and a "doing part." Of course, this is an oversimplified explanation of how the brain functions, but it will help you to better understand what may be occurring.

In a person with OCD, the worry part of the brain is where the OCD "lives." It is the OCD "command center." The worry part of the brain sends fear messages to the doing part of the brain. These fear messages contain warnings of horrible things to come. The messages come in the form of worries, the "What if?" and "Oh no!" types of thoughts. Examples include "What if I left the iron on and plugged in, and what if it causes a fire?" or "Oh, no! I touched the handle of that shopping cart and now I'm contaminated." The command center of the worry part of the brain sends these messages to the doing part of the brain, and the doing part is then responsible for formulating a plan of action or behavioral response

Let's look at an everyday example of how this aspect of brain functioning likely works in you, assuming you don't have OCD. You're cooking dinner one night and your arm accidentally gets too close to the burner on the stove. The command center of your brain would instantaneously respond by sending the message, "Oh no! My hand is too close to the stove and it hurts! I'm getting burned!" The doing part of the brain would then execute a behavioral response, such as quickly pulling back your hand to avoid getting burned further. In essence, the worry part of the brain sends a justified fear message, "Uh oh! We have a problem here!" and the doing part is responsible for fixing the problem or averting the feared outcome.

Now, let's look at an example of how this might play out for someone with OCD fears of contamination. Let's say that the person just opened the door to a public bathroom. The command center would then send out fear messages to the doing part. "I touched that door handle! What if there were germs or bacteria on that handle? Now they may be all over my hands! And what if I just leave the germs on my hands, and later on I forget about it and put my hand or fingers in my mouth? I could get very sick. That would be horrible!" The command center has now sounded the alarm, and the doing part must respond in a way that addresses that fear. In the person who has OCD fears of germs, the response is typically a ritual aimed at reducing the threat of contamination or illness. In this example, the doing part of the brain is likely to respond by initiating a hand washing or decontamination ritual, or by seeking reassurance.

Each time the doing part of the brain appeases the worry part of the brain by initiating a ritual, the worry part of the brain becomes stronger and more demanding. As the worry part of the brain becomes stronger, the command center sends out more and more fear messages. Oftentimes, these fear messages include greater threats of feared outcomes and consequences. Just as you can turn up the volume on the radio, the volume and intensity of the OCD fear messages become louder and harder to ignore. The result for the person with OCD is a growing experience of anxiety or impending doom accompanied by a greater sense of urgency to reduce the fear by engaging in a ritual.

UNCERTAINTY IS THE ENEMY

It's the person's inability to tolerate or accept uncertainty that underlies OCD, and it's the pursuit of attaining 100 percent certainty that drives rituals and feeds OCD. People who have OCD want to be absolutely certain that their "what if?" OCD fears will not come true. They have difficulty tolerating the anxiety and uncertainty of the unanswered "what ifs?" and so they feel compelled to engage in rituals in an attempt to attain certainty. Common certainties pursued by people with OCD include the following:

- "Nothing bad will happen to me or someone I care about."

- "Nothing bad happened or will happen as a result of something I did or failed to do."

- "I did not offend another person."

- "I will not act on that violent thought."

- "That particular thought was meaningless or meant _____."

- "I did not blaspheme or otherwise disrespect God."

The inability to feel absolutely certain about something is an everyday experience that most of us don't question. The fact that we don't question these uncertainties reflects our acceptance of them. Assumptions that we make every day also reflect our acceptance of the uncertainties with which we live. Take a moment to think about someone close to you. Where is he or she right now? Is the person alive and well? How do you know for sure? Is it possible that something tragic has happened since you last spoke to the person?

The reality is that you don't really know *factually*, for certain, that your loved one is alive and well. However, you are likely willing to settle for the assumption that he or she is alive and well. Although you might feel a knee-jerk reaction of anxiety to the thought and resulting uncertainty, you probably feel *emotionally* certain enough that you do not *have* to call the person immediately to make certain of his or her well-being. You can attempt to use logic or reassure yourself that you probably would have been notified if a problem existed. In essence, you are willing to pretend and act *as if* your loved one is okay until it is proven otherwise. You are willing to accept uncertainty without feeling compelled to prove or disprove a particular possibility. You can tolerate not being 100 percent certain at this time. Use the following Living with Uncertainty chart to list uncertainties that you live with all the time. As you do this exercise, think about the uncertainties you live with every day. You may not often think in these terms. This chart gives you an opportunity to experience the thinking patterns frequently experienced by people with OCD.

Living with Uncertainty

List some uncertainties or assumptions that you're able to live with and accept in day-to-day life.

1. _____

_____

2. _____

_____

3. _____

_____

4. _____

_____

List some "what if?" types of thoughts related to your uncertainties and assumptions. For example, "What if my son was in an accident and is in the emergency room?"

1. _____

2. _____

3. _____

4. _____

5. _____

6. _____

7. _____

8. _____

People with OCD can accept the uncertainties of life as long as these are areas of life that are not tied up in their OCD fears. For example, if fearing for their loved one's well-being is not part of their OCD fears, most people with OCD would respond to the question of a loved one's safety in much the same way you did—with a knee-jerk anxiety reaction followed by the ability to dismiss the question and need for certainty. But when confronted with the uncertainty of an OCD fear or with accepting the real possibility that a feared outcome may actually occur, the attainment of 100 percent factual certainty becomes the required goal. Without 100 percent factual certainty, there's no alleviation of the distressing experience of emotional uncertainty. At the same time, it is the emotional uncertainty that fuels OCD rituals and the pursuit of factual certainty.

Let's look closer at the roles of distress, anxiety, and the intolerance of uncertainty in the OCD moment. When her OCD was more severe, Cherry was haunted by fear that she would cause a fire if she weren't "careful enough." Many mornings, after leaving for work, Cherry had thoughts and doubts such as "I'm pretty sure I checked that the coffeepot (or stove, computer, lights, etc.) was turned off before I left the house, but what if I really didn't? Or what if I didn't check thoroughly enough? What if I was distracted when I checked, and I somehow missed the fact that it was still on? What if I really turned it on instead of off, and then the coffee pot blows up because it's empty, and somehow causes a fire? Maybe I'm remembering when I checked it yesterday and didn't even check it today!

In an effort to alleviate the distress and anxiety, Cherry would feel driven to obtain certainty through some kind of action or ritual. Rituals in this situation included self-reassurance and mental reviewing in an effort to recall details of going into the kitchen and checking the coffeepot. Sometimes rituals involved returning home and checking the coffeepot yet another time. If family members were home, Cherry often called home and asked them to check and make certain the coffeepot, stove, or computer was off. One time, she called a neighbor who had a key to the house and asked her to go over and check the coffeepot. Regardless of the *form* of the ritual, most rituals are performed in an attempt to prove 100 percent certainty.

Sometimes rituals are driven by the need to be certain that they have the perfect plan in place and are prepared, just in case the "what if?" occurs. They take the old Boy Scout motto, "Be prepared," to a higher level. Rather than responding to a problem if and when it occurs, people with OCD often try to head the problem off at the pass. They spend a considerable amount of time trying to figure out solutions to an overwhelming and infinite number of combinations of "what ifs?" before they even occur. For example, in an effort to plan for the "what if?" of no one being at home to check the appliances, Cherry planned ahead and made certain her neighbor had a key and was willing to enter her house to check various appliances when needed without rebuking her.

So far, the logic behind the rituals seems to make sense. If you don't know something for certain, and you feel emotional distress as a result, you take steps to find out for certain. But when it comes to OCD and trying to be certain in the OCD moment, logic no longer prevails. In fact, the use of logic can actually add fuel to the OCD fire. The goal of attaining certainty on this type of question is fraught with confusion. The infinite number of "what ifs?" combines and multiplies exponentially.

The growth of thoughts is what increases and feeds the anxiety. There are too many "what ifs?" to fathom or consider. Every "what if?" always has a multitude of "what ifs?" that follows. Trying to address each and every "what if?" quickly becomes overwhelming. Trying to answer the "what if?" questions is like digging a hole in the sand that keeps filling in on itself.

Learning to Live with Uncertainty

So how does a person with OCD learn to live with uncertainty? What exactly does that mean when we're talking about recovery from OCD? The goals for someone learning to live with uncertainty are as follows:

- Facing the anxiety and distress of the obsessions and "what ifs?" without resorting to a ritual.

- Stopping the voluntary habit of looking for certainty.

- Avoiding getting trapped in the futile search for certainty.

- Being able to say, "I don't know . . . I may never know . . . but I can learn to live with not knowing."

The best way to explain *how* to start learning to live with uncertainty is to describe *what* needs to stop occurring—the rituals. Anything designed to neutralize or decrease the anxiety of an obsession interferes with the process of learning to live with uncertainty. Oftentimes it seems as though the rituals are voluntary, but sometimes the rituals are sneaky enough to seem automatic. Regardless, the benefits of cognitive behavioral therapy become evident when the person with OCD purposely prevents the ritual. As a family member, it's important for you to understand how rituals feed the futile search for certainty. This will help you think about OCD moments differently and thus support your loved one differently. Understanding OCD will improve your strategies for living with and loving someone with OCD. You can learn more about the concept of uncertainty and OCD by reading *Freedom from Obsessive-Compulsive Disorder: A Personalized Recovery Program for Living with Uncertainty* (Grayson 2003).

FEEDING OCD

As family members observe their loved one with OCD caught in a cycle of obsessions and compulsions, it's natural and intuitive to want to help. But in the case of OCD, some helping behaviors that seem perfectly reasonable at first actually become food for the OCD to grow on! As OCD is fed, it grows and becomes stronger and hungrier. It's never satisfied. Slowly and over time, the natural and intuitive help of family members may unknowingly become an active part of the OCD cycle. It's as if OCD lies in wait and seizes any opportunity to use your intuition and good intent against you and your loved one. Its goal is to pull you into its grasp, in much the same way that it took hold of your loved one.

This workbook will teach you more about this inadvertent "feeding trap" that OCD has laid. By providing strategic help and support, you'll be able to avoid the trap. By giving strategic support, you will work with your loved one against the OCD while weakening its grip on everyone involved.

HIDING BEHIND NORMALCY

There may be some situations where you don't even realize that you are part of an OCD moment. This is because your loved one may put much effort into hiding the rituals or symptoms of OCD. Some rituals are masked by their subtlety. Others may be masked as normal types of behaviors or requests that you would never think to question. This is especially true in the case of avoidance rituals.

Avoidance rituals are intended to reduce the anxiety and distress of OCD. They may help your loved one avoid certain situations or objects all together. For instance, Cherry sometimes asked her husband to check the coffeepot or stove on the way out of the house. This request seems innocent enough on the surface. After all, it appears to be a normal and typical request that we have all probably made of others. Now let's uncover the trap that OCD has set. What if she was forced to directly confront the situation? She could become stuck in a ritual of repeatedly checking the coffeepot or stove before leaving the house. Cherry's husband was acting as an unknowing accomplice to her avoidance. OCD is *that* sneaky and tricky! By recruiting her husband to check, she successfully avoided the obsession of not being certain the appliance was off, and thus avoided the fear and distress of being responsible for anything bad that might occur (e.g., causing a fire) as a result of the appliance being left on.

Your loved one's attempts to procrastinate on certain tasks or responsibilities in order to delay the associated distress are other forms of avoidance rituals. It's important to recognize that any form of avoidance is nothing more than a ritual—a purposeful omission designed to avert anxiety and doubt. Remember, any ritual, whether it involves a purposeful act or the purposeful omission of an act, only serves to feed the OCD.

HIDDEN RITUALS

Some rituals may remain hidden from you because they occur within the mind and are associated with no observable physical behavior. These are referred to as *mental rituals*, and they serve the same purpose as any other form of ritual. They are intended to decrease the anxiety, distress, and uncertainty caused by the obsession.

Mental rituals include such things as counting, repetitive prayers, and thinking a "good" thought to undo a "bad" thought. Mental rituals can also include repeatedly recalling or reviewing a situation or conversation in order to be certain about something or in order to "figure something out." Another form of mental rituals occurs when the person tries to reassure him- or herself with such thoughts as "It must be okay that I touched that door handle. Mom would have told me to wash my hands if it was contaminated or dangerous," or "There's no need to worry! The coffeepot must be off. I checked it three times."

WHY CAN'T THEY JUST STOP THESE BEHAVIORS?

There may be times when you question whether your loved one has control over this seemingly bizarre behavior. It's natural for this question to arise because many people with debilitating OCD symptoms that affect some areas of life are very high functioning and accomplished in other areas. People with OCD are often more than capable of maintaining a job or professional career, participating in rigorous academic programs, pursuing extracurricular activities or sports, and maintaining friendships and intimate relationships. But at the very same time, the person can act in ways that seem bizarre, unreasonable, and irrational. Watching people function in such opposing and contradictory manners can cause great confusion and misunderstanding. Thus, it's common for family members to question, "Why is he acting this way? Why can't he just stop this ridiculous behavior? Why can't he control himself better? Is he going crazy?"

Rest assured that having OCD doesn't cause people to go crazy in the sense that you might fear. People who are "going crazy" or "losing touch with reality" often don't recognize that their thoughts or behaviors are irrational. When confronted by others, they'll vehemently defend their thoughts, beliefs, and behaviors. In contrast, outside of the immediate OCD moment, people who have OCD usually *do* agree that their fears and behaviors are irrational, silly, or at least unnecessary. They'll simply explain, "I know that it doesn't make sense, but I still feel like I have to do it!"

As a concerned and loving family member, you're not the only one to question the craziness of life with OCD. Often, people who have OCD also fear that they are "going crazy" or feel like they're "losing their mind." How else can they make sense of their obsessional thoughts and uncertainties, repetitive rituals, and emotional turmoil? They feel out of control because they can't respond to their own logic or the logic of family members. During the OCD moment, uncertainty and emotions rule over logic. They *know* that their rituals make no sense, yet they *feel* as though they must do them anyway. Outside of the OCD moment, when logic once again prevails, they may fear for their sanity.

Until they learn new ways through cognitive behavioral therapy to handle uncertainty and OCD symptoms, people with OCD can't always just "stop" bizarre or irrational behaviors at will. With all the suffering and anguish they experience as a result of living with OCD, surely they would "just stop" if they could. It's important to realize that, at least at this point and at this time, they're not able to respond to anxiety and OCD any differently. By reading this workbook, you're beginning to develop a better understanding of the "inner workings" of OCD that give rise to the vicious cycle of OCD. Armed with this knowledge, you'll be better prepared for supporting and loving someone with OCD.

Summary

For people with OCD, the inability to tolerate or accept uncertainty results in obsessions and anxiety, and the pursuit of attaining 100 percent certainty drives the rituals. Learning to live with uncertainty is an important part of breaking free from OCD. This can only be done by facing the anxiety and distress of obsessions without resorting to rituals, stopping the voluntary habit of looking for uncertainty, and avoiding getting trapped in the futile search for certainty.

It's only natural for family members to want to help their loved one who is struggling with OCD feel safe. They get caught in the cycles of obsessions and rituals, providing help the only way they know how. They try to provide certainty by offering reassurance or by participating in rituals. At first, the helping behaviors seem quite reasonable, but they feed the OCD, and OCD is never satisfied. Over time, the participation of family members in OCD rituals grows. You and your loved one may both feel that you've fallen into "feeding traps" that OCD has laid. You may feel frustrated, even angry, as you've tried futilely to escape the traps. These are common feelings. We'll help you to recognize these OCD traps and develop strategies for breaking free from them.

Chapter 4

Support the Person,
Not the OCD

The fact that you have discovered this book and have read this far means you are trying to understand your loved one as he or she struggles with OCD. You're likely also searching for answers to your own struggle to live with someone with OCD. Throughout the following pages, we will address many of the issues and conflicts that families commonly experience when a loved one is living with OCD. You will also gain a better understanding of how your family member's OCD symptoms affect family interactions and, likewise, how family interactions affect OCD symptoms.

FAMILY AS AN AGENT OF CHANGE

OCD often impacts the entire family, resulting in tremendous confusion and conflict among everyone. It's important to remember, however, that everyone is probably trying to cope with the situation as best they can. Through choices made by each family member trying to cope with OCD in the home, OCD can become a family disorder. Fortunately, getting well can become a family effort. This chapter will help you understand how your efforts as a concerned family member can contribute to a successful outcome for your loved one's individual therapy.

This chapter is designed to help you learn more about how your actions can impact your loved one's OCD. It will help you change your reactions to your loved one so that your responses are helpful in a therapeutic and positive way. You'll learn how to help stop the spread and growth of unhealthy OCD behaviors that occur as a result of giving in to the demands of OCD. It will help you view yourself as an agent of change. This will allow you to navigate your way through the feelings of powerlessness and confusion that you may be feeling now. These are common feelings among those dealing with someone with OCD. Family members can feel helpless as they watch their spouse or child in the depths of suffering and struggling with obsessive-compulsive disorder. Likewise, people with OCD often feel powerless and helpless in their OCD world. Families are frequently confused about what it means to be supportive, helpful, and therapeutic.

Many families report that they feel like they have tried everything. You may have tried to point out the irrationality of the OCD fears or tried to be convincing that the worries were unfounded. You may be taking part in OCD rituals in order to keep the peace or to avoid an argument. Sometimes these attempts appear to work. At other times, they seem to make the situation even worse. The frustration that follows often increases family stress and has a disruptive impact on everyone involved. These responses can also impact your loved one in ways that you certainly were not intending. They may even increase his or her OCD symptoms. This chapter willl help you understand how this can occur.

Acknowledging Feelings about OCD

Family members experience a wide range of emotions about OCD. They can feel confused, guilty, fearful, angry, doubtful, disappointed, and distraught. They're often filled with heartache, and they may blame themselves or feel blamed by others and burdened by guilt, hostility, or resentment. You might be feeling overwhelmed and helpless, having tried everything to help your family member. Perhaps your attempts have been ineffective or rejected by your loved one. When this happens, feelings of helplessness and despair grow.

Below are some common negative feelings experienced when loving someone with OCD. Check off the ones you are experiencing now.

- ☐ Fear

- ☐ Doubt

- ☐ Anger

- ☐ Guilt

- ☐ Disappointment

- ☐ Loneliness and feeling alone

- ☐ Isolation

- ☐ Distress

- ☐ Overwhelmed

- ☐ Powerlessness

- ☐ Helplessness

- ☐ Blamed by others

- ☐ Hostility

- ☐ Resentment

- ☐ Despair

- ☐ Frustration

- ☐ Confusion

Family members often feel frustrated after repeatedly engaging in accommodating behaviors. They may express their frustration through resentment and hostility toward the person during the OCD episode. They might criticize their loved one for ritualizing and for "listening" to the fearful obsessive thoughts. These reactions to the demands of OCD make it seem like family members are blaming the person with OCD for his or her compulsive behaviors. Although family members often report being apologetic after these incidents, such criticism contributes to the person's shame and embarrassment. Feelings toward OCD and feelings toward each other become confused for everyone involved. Joan's mother helped her daughter get up early every morning to allow time for Joan's checking to make certain everything was in the bag Joan took to work. As she drove Joan to work, however, she would berate her for being "ridiculous" and wasting time. Then she'd express her worries about how Joan would ever be able to live on her own.

Many families understand that their accommodating behaviors are not helpful, yet feelings of helplessness and powerlessness lead them to "go with what they know." They don't want to see their spouse or child continue to suffer. Soon, OCD is ruling their lives as well. OCD becomes the center of the family's life, and everyone starts living by OCD's rules.

Other family members may be resentful of the attention, albeit negative, that the person with OCD receives. Family members can become overly involved or, alternatively, too distanced from each other. Parents may share mutual beliefs and feelings about how to deal with their child's OCD or differ widely in their reactions to the OCD. Or they may vary their reactions unpredictably between compassion and hostility. Meanwhile the family dysfunction and chaos grows.

Family members may also become socially isolated as, out of desperation, they pull away from others. It's difficult enough to acknowledge these painful feelings to yourself, let alone risk the embarrassment of sharing your feelings with others. You may be carrying these emotional burdens alone because you don't know any other families affected by OCD. But it's important for you to realize that these are normal reactions to seeing a family member behave uncontrollably and do unusual things. These are also normal reactions to seeing the pain and struggle of a loved one living with OCD.

It's natural to feel the other person's pain. It's this distress that has motivated you to seek help and to read this book. Remember that feeling distressed is where you begin but not where you should stay. Acknowledging negative feelings is an important first step toward choosing healthier, more supportive responses to your loved one's OCD.

HEALTHY, SUPPORTIVE RESPONSES

Healthy family support begins with choosing effective ways to respond to your loved one's OCD. By working with your loved one over time, you can help put OCD in its rightfully insignificant place in your life and in your family's life. OCD does not have to take over your life and your home. If it feels like it already has, it does not have to remain that way any longer.

What does family support mean? Support means different things at different times for different people. Sometimes being supportive can feel stressful. At other times, providing support can feel uplifting and freeing for everyone involved. In order to be as supportive as possible of your loved one's recovery from OCD, you need to become aware of some of the dilemmas that may arise. But first, let's address how you envision support. Complete the Your Meaning of Support chart. Make copies for other family members to complete. You may want to discuss your answers.

Your Meaning of Support

What does the word "support" mean to you?

_____

_____

_____

_____

When you need help or support, what do you want from your loved ones?

_____

_____

_____

_____

Has there been a time in the past when you needed help or support from others, yet you found yourself feeling alone or misunderstood? Describe how you felt.

_____

_____

_____

_____

What kinds of struggles do you experience while trying to be supportive of your loved one with OCD?

_____

_____

_____

_____

FOLLOWING YOUR INSTINCTS

You probably answered some of the questions above based on your instincts. Unfortunately, following your instincts on how to help your loved one with OCD is not always what best supports recovery from the grips of OCD. Instincts are often driven by emotion and result in responses such as giving in, reassuring, or debating with the person with OCD. While these reactions may seem to get you through the moment at hand, they work to make OCD symptoms stronger. Giving in, reassuring, or debating are not constructive ways to help decrease the symptoms of OCD. These efforts at support are actually OCD accommodations in disguise.

Accommodating family reactions makes OCD symptoms stronger. Cognitive behavioral therapy, specifically ERP, requires that the individual take risks. Responses such as giving in, reassuring, and debating only work to undermine the risk taking required for recovery. Throughout the therapy process, your support of your loved one's risk-taking behaviors is of the utmost importance. Therefore, you need to become aware of how your reactions may unintentionally work against the goals and outcome of the cognitive behavioral therapy. Just as important is learning how to effectively support the battle against OCD while avoiding the mistakes and pitfalls that can work against both of you.

In trying to help a loved one function and get through a typical day, family members may assist in rituals or even perform the rituals in an effort to avoid rocking the boat. Sometimes family members report taking over responsibilities in the hopes that it will somehow make things better or easier for the person with OCD. But by doing these things, well-intentioned family members unknowingly undermine the loved one's risk-taking potential. The typical person doesn't realize that these choices interfere with recovery.

Many family members initially express concern about changing their reactions to their loved one's "OCD needs." These changes may seem contrary to their own instincts or what seems to be helpful in most normal situations. But support for someone with OCD is different from support for someone who is depressed or going through a crisis; it is less intuitive and more strategic. Remember, any of your reactions that undermines the goal of exposure and risk taking works against recovery from OCD. And if you're not supporting ERP and risk taking, then you're helping to make the OCD symptoms stronger.

OCD makes many demands that directly impact the roles of family members and the choices they make while trying to help. You may need to redefine your role in your loved one's recovery. Your new role will involve responses that are strategic and supportive of risk taking rather than reactions that are unintentionally counterproductive and interfere with the treatment process. Family member support is related to a successful outcome in the treatment of OCD.

ACCOMMODATION: THE OCD WELCOME WAGON

Let's take a closer look at the natural, intuitive approaches to supporting your loved one with OCD. These are often accommodating behaviors and can be likened to an OCD welcome wagon. You essentially invite OCD into your home and make it comfortable through your accommodations. Just as you try to make an old friend or other guest feel comfortable and welcome in your home, you extend yourself to OCD and its demands. It's as if you cater to OCD as you would a guest: "What can I do for you? What can I get for you? Anything you need, just let me know." The more comfortable you make the OCD, the longer it wants to stay in your home.

Accommodation occurs whenever you behave or react to OCD symptoms in ways that can undermine the therapeutic goal of exposure and risk taking. It is a way of paying undue respect to OCD and its demands on you and your loved one. Accommodating supports OCD, not the person with OCD. By changing these behaviors, you are making a conscious decision to support your loved one instead of the OCD. You may actually act as if you're scared of your family member's OCD, when you may really be fearful of his or her reaction to the obsessions. Or perhaps you're really trying to protect your family member from the unfounded fear.

Accommodating behaviors occur quite naturally and make sense at the time. Your attempts at helping are genuine and come from the heart. They sometimes give you a sense of control over a virtually uncontrollable situation—a situation that has left you feeling fearful, helpless, and exhausted. No "small" accommodation is ever truly small, however. Each accommodation serves as food for the OCD and serves to help OCD grow stronger.

Accommodation Traps

The accommodation traps described here are common to many families struggling to be helpful and supportive. The goal here is to provide you with a sense of community and help you feel less alone with the impact of this disorder. You may identify with some of these descriptions of others as you sympathize with the pitfalls and frustrations of challenging OCD moments. You are not alone in your struggles and challenges. You can learn from other people's difficulties and increase awareness of your own behaviors and interactions that tangle you up with OCD. The scenarios below also cover the messages that accommodations communicate to people with OCD regarding their own abilities to cope. For each trap, you'll be asked to relate it to your own experience.

Accommodation Trap 1: Providing Reassurance

How often do you find yourself telling your loved one something to make him or her feel better, such as when you're asked the same questions over and over again? "Yes, I am sure that you checked that the stove is turned off," "Yes, I'm sure you washed your hands well enough," "Yes, I'm sure that you didn't make a mistake," "Yes I am sure you said the numbers in the right order," or "Yes, I'm sure they do not have AIDS." In these cases, you are repeatedly reassuring your loved one. He or she may ask you the exact same question over and over again or reword the question in many different ways. Sometimes your response even becomes part of the ritual so that there are rules about how your reassurance should be worded.

Reassurance consists of convincing your loved one that an obsessive thought or fear is false and will not occur. Likewise, your loved one may seek reassurance that the ritual itself was performed correctly and/or that the feared outcome will not happen. Reassurance reinforces the fear messages sent by the worry part of the brain. The worry part demands that your loved one make absolutely certain that terrible consequences will not occur. You help provide that demanded reassurance and certainty.

Joan had extensive prayer rituals. Her OCD told her that she needed to specifically name all of her family members in her prayers each night. OCD fear messages also told her that if she accidentally left a family member out, then God would not protect that person from bad things happening. The outcomes she feared were that something bad would happen to someone she cared about, it would be her fault, and she would have to live with tremendous guilt for the rest of her life. She sometimes felt so frustrated that she had one of her parents listen to make sure she had included everyone in her prayers, and thus that the ritual was performed correctly. She'd ask such questions as, "Do you think that if I accidentally forget to mention someone in my prayers that God would understand and still protect everyone? If I do forget someone and then something bad happens, does that mean it would be all my fault?" These questions are examples of how she sought reassurance that her feared outcomes would not come true.

Describe an incident where you may have provided reassurance.

_____

_____

_____

_____

Intuitively, your instincts might lead you to question why you should withhold the reassurance from someone. Stop and think of reasons why such reassurance may be harmful. How might your simple reassurance have been harmful?

_____

_____

_____

_____

When trapped in the cycle of reassurance, you may feel like you're talking to someone who just isn't listening or is of limited intelligence. A more accurate way to think about this trap is that you and your loved are creating a skip on a record player, and one of you needs to move the needle ahead to continue the song. To move ahead, you both must recognize the reassurance trap for what it truly is and agree that risk taking and exposure is the way to move past the moment. Remember, when you give reassurance, you reduce the risks of uncertainty that have to be confronted head-on. By reducing these risks, you feed the OCD.

You may find yourself trying incessantly to drill your loved one with logic against the unfounded fear. You're then struggling with the OCD rather than your loved one; they're also struggling with the OCD. You're trying to reason logically and debate with someone who is reasoning by feelings alone in that OCD moment. Family members report the frustration of trying to rationalize away fears, which sometimes will "work" for a short period of time. The unfortunate fact that rationalizing sometimes appears to work in the short run only serves to reinforce its use. The next time you and your loved one are in a similar OCD situation, you're more likely to react with a rational debate or argument instead of supporting your loved one to do more risk taking. Debating works along the same lines as giving reassurance.

Describe an incident when you have attempted to debate or rationalize away your loved one's OCD fears.

_____

_____

_____

_____

How might debating or rationalizing have been harmful?

_____

_____

_____

_____

Accommodation Trap 2: Avoidance

How often do you find yourself going through your normal routine only to stop suddenly out of fear that you might trigger your loved one's obsessions or ritualizing? Marilyn's family members would avoid entering the room if she was cleaning because interrupting her cleaning rituals meant she would start her frantic cleaning all over again. Sometimes this meant having to eat meals in a different part of the house if she was in the kitchen, or sitting in the basement and waiting until she was finished using several parts of the house during her rituals. Joan's parents would avoid driving past a local cemetery because the sight of the cemetery would trigger her OCD rituals. At times, this meant having to go many miles out of their way in order to avoid the cemetery. They would anticipate their driving route ahead of time to plan accordingly.

Describe a situation when you have avoided a certain place, person, thing, or topic of conversation for fear of triggering an OCD moment.

_____

_____

_____

_____

Stop and think of reasons why your avoidance may have been harmful.

_____

_____

_____

_____

You may find that you are refraining from doing or saying things that trigger symptoms, but avoidance is just another way of giving OCD more respect than it deserves. You are not limiting the OCD, only allowing it to lie in wait to seize the next unpredictable moment.

Accommodation Trap 3: Participating in Time-Consuming Rituals

Melinda's family was so intricately involved in their daughter's rituals that she could not perform them independently. Her father was very helpful with the rituals, such as reassuring her that her counting was done perfectly, offering to decontaminate foods for her, and saying magical word combinations before eating. If Dad messed up the ritual, they had to start over. The ritualizing could take entire days to complete and meals, as well as other parts of daily functioning, were sometimes postponed until the rituals were complete. Melinda's parents were fearful for their daughter's well-being as they were getting older and weaker. How would Melinda survive without them? Would she starve to death? They believed they had to participate in the rituals to keep her alive. This is a severe example of how OCD can grow slowly, sneakily, and insidiously until rituals are requiring extreme amounts of participation. Initially, you may start helping out with the ritual to make it go faster, but eventually, you may become a necessary element of the ritual.

When Cherry's OCD was at its worst, her checking rituals often caused the family to leave home late for social obligations and commitments. In an effort to help reduce his wife's anxiety and to ensure they would leave home on time, Cherry's husband Jim began "helping out" with the checking. While she waited in the car, he checked things and locked the door. Cherry had now transferred responsibility to her husband. Even if, as she suspected, he had not checked everything "correctly and completely," she wouldn't feel it was her fault if a disaster occurred.

How often do you find yourself participating in your loved one's rituals? Describe a situation in which you were observing or participating in the ritual.

_____

_____

_____

_____

List reasons why participating in rituals may have been harmful.

_____

_____

_____

_____

Accommodation Trap 4: Assistance with Decisions or Simple Tasks

Family members often report that they feel like they need to take over making choices or decisions for their loved one. As with all other forms of accommodating, assisting in decision making undermines the goal of risk taking. In this instance, the risk is that the decision he or she makes may turn out to be the wrong or least perfect decision.

A person with OCD may become caught in the grocery store in a wave of indecisiveness, unable to complete the shopping trip, questioning each item and trying to make the best and perfect decision. "Should I buy this cereal or that one? Should I buy a bulk package because it's less money per box? But then there might be too much . . . or maybe I should get it at the other store. It's on sale now; what if there's a better sale next week?" A person can cycle in obsessive indecisiveness on whether or not to purchase just one item or can obsess about every item needed during the grocery trip. This is often an attempt to avoid regret about a decision, the possibility that the best and most perfect decision about a simple, everyday purchase won't be made.

Family members often find themselves assisting their loved one with everyday tasks. Some parents find themselves cleaning their adult child's room because the contamination fears would cause the person to spend hours cleaning over and over. Husbands and wives often take over duties their spouses once did to save time and frustration. It's much easier to mow the lawn, clean the toilet, or open the mail than watch a loved one suffer. For some family members, laundry day becomes an onerous task as the person with OCD insists on elaborately organizing clothing by color, style, and other categories. Folding and putting clothes away could take the person with OCD four times as long and cause marked distress. The simple task of placing clothes in drawers becomes complicated and time-consuming.

How often do you find yourself helping your family member make the simplest of decisions, such as in what order to complete the day's errands? Sometimes a person with OCD can get caught up in trying to figure out the most perfect, effective, and efficient way of completing the day's errands and tasks. Are there times when you take over and make these decisions so that you can end the indecisiveness and anguish or can just move on with the day?

Describe a situation in which you became very involved with your loved one's decisions.

_____

_____

_____

_____

Describe a situation in which you became very involved in completing a simple task for your loved one with OCD.

_____

_____

_____

_____

Looking back, was your overinvolvement helpful or harmful?

_____

_____

_____

_____

Accommodation Trap 5: Modification of Your Work, Family, or Social Responsibilities and Routines

Linda's mother could no longer wash laundry in the morning because her daughter used all the hot water showering. Marilyn's husband had to change clothes in the garage, then wash his hands and feet with a solution of bleach and water before taking a shower as soon as he came home from work each day while Marilyn "decontaminated" his clothes in the laundry. Mario's father accommodated Mario's frequent hand washing and contamination fears at work in the family business. Mario did paperwork and had little contact with customers. Mario required that his father clean his hands before entering Mario's office since they may have been in contact with customers.

Many families speak of feeling isolated because they can't spend time with friends or invite others over because it would interfere with OCD rituals. Some people report that they refrain from physical contact with "contaminated" friends or family members or that they rarely or secretly visit other relatives because of their loved one's contamination obsessions. One woman reported that she had not seen her aging mother in three years because her daughter's OCD fears included the fear that her grandmother was contaminated.

Do you find that you often change your schedule or routine for the day because it might interfere with taking care of your loved one's OCD concerns? Describe a situation in which you modified your work responsibilities for your loved one with OCD.

_____

_____

_____

_____

Describe a situation in which you modified your family responsibilities for your loved one with OCD.

_____

_____

_____

_____

Describe a situation in which you modified your social responsibilities for your loved one with OCD.

_____

_____

_____

_____

Describe a situation in which you modified your typical routine for your loved one with OCD.

_____

_____

_____

_____

How do you feel when you modify your responsibilities or routine to accommodate OCD?

_____

_____

_____

_____

Accommodation Trap 6: Assuming Your Loved One's Responsibilities

Alisha was afraid her husband Deon would lose his job because he was late leaving the house so often. She rearranged her schedule so that she could leave the house after Deon, promising him that she'd check the stove, computer, and lights, just as he usually did, then lock the door carefully. Sometimes assuming a person's responsibilities is tied in with the avoidance behavior discussed earlier in this chapter.

Some families have reported that the daily mail delivery is a sore area, ripe for avoidance. They may sort mail before their loved one, a checker, can find bills that need to be paid. Another family member will pay the bills to avoid the inevitable ritualizing over writing the check correctly or properly sealing the envelope without forgetting something or making an embarrassing mistake. Marilyn's husband did all the grocery shopping because Marilyn would perform several decontamination rituals for each item before entering the house, which often took several hours. The perishable food was often spoiled by the time she was ready to put it in the refrigerator. Family members can become trapped in this form of accommodating, often out of guilt or because they feel bad for their loved one.

Have you made numerous exceptions or assumed your loved one's responsibilities because of his or her OCD symptoms? Describe a situation in which you expected less from your loved one.

Describe a situation in which you assumed your loved one's responsibility because of his or her OCD symptoms.

How do you feel about assuming these additional responsibilities?

Accommodation Trap 7: Tolerating Abnormal Behaviors or Conditions

Families have reported that they cannot access their kitchens for cooking and must cook at their neighbor's home because of their loved one's OCD-related hoarding or they cannot use their cooking utensils due to their loved one's contamination fears. Sandy's family members could barely walk through her house because it was so cluttered with hoarded and seemingly useless items. The odor from the almost one hundred cats she had collected was almost unbearable.

Mario's father was embarrassed the rare times Mario had contact with customers. Mario refused to shake hands and was fearful someone would touch him, so he kept his hands in his pockets or firmly by his side. If anyone touched him or if he touched something he considered contaminated, he would walk quickly to the bathroom to wash his hands. Since he rarely explained where he was going, bewildered customers were left to wonder what went wrong.

Do you find that you tolerate embarrassing or unusual behaviors? Describe embarrassing or unusual behaviors you tolerate from your loved one.

_____

_____

_____

_____

Describe uncomfortable or noxious living conditions that you tolerate in your home.

_____

_____

_____

_____

Do you recognize that these conditions are not normal, yet feel you must accept them as a part of your way of living? Are you ashamed to have guests visit your home? Describe a situation in which you felt ashamed to have visitors in your home.

_____

_____

_____

_____

THINKING DIFFERENTLY ABOUT SUPPORT

The above examples have introduced you to different ways family members try to help and support their loved ones with OCD. As you have seen, families can inadvertently fall into accommodating traps in their desire to help. Did you find these examples and descriptions similar to your own situation? Are you thinking differently or in new ways about your own situation? How so?

_____

_____

_____

_____

How Common Is Accommodation?

Intuitively, we all act in similar ways in an effort to soothe our loved one's fears or calm his or her nervousness. But when we try to soothe our loved one's OCD fears "intuitively," we may in fact be inadvertently feeding the OCD. One reason for this is that OCD is very sneaky. It makes it very difficult to recognize that these behaviors increase the symptoms of OCD. Although accommodating responses seem to work at first, they usually lose their power as the obsessions and compulsions continue. The usual result is that you find yourself reassuring more often and more repeatedly, or you find yourself participating in rituals that grow more complex and time-consuming.

Identifying your own accommodating responses is important for many reasons. The way you respond to or accommodate your loved one's OCD symptoms impacts everyone involved—your loved one, yourself, and your other family members. If you have been accommodating your loved one's OCD, you aren't alone. You aren't the only one to try to solve these problems in this manner, and you are not the only one to try to care for your loved one in this way. In a recent study, almost 60 percent of families who had a loved one suffering from OCD participated in or observed rituals, avoided objects or situations that the loved one feared, or provided reassurance regarding an unfounded fear (Calvacoressi et al., 1995).

Four Conclusions about Accommodating Behaviors

Here are four conclusions that can be drawn from a review of recent research and our clinical experience about the types of accommodating traps we discussed earlier.

1. There is a significant relationship between accommodating behaviors, OCD symptom severity, and individual and family functioning.

The more family members participate in accommodating behaviors, the more severe symptoms become and the lower the level of the functioning becomes for the loved one with OCD. Functioning could mean the ability to make decisions, perform tasks and activities, or operate well at school, work, or home. This might mean functioning at a lower capacity or less than expected by others.

Here's an example of how accommodating, symptom severity, and functioning operate together. You may find yourself reassuring your loved one repeatedly. Despite the reassurance, the same types of questions constantly arise. You are feeding a particular OCD fear or obsession. Your loved one asks for reassurance in hopes that your answer will provide certainty. The more you provide the reassurance, the more your loved one will rely on your reassurance to calm fears and gain certainty. The more your loved one depends on reassurance to soothe anxiety and distress, the more it impacts your loved one's ability to function.

2. The more family members participate in accommodating behaviors, the greater the level of family dysfunction and negative attitudes toward the person with OCD.

Negative feelings can drive a wedge in your relationship. Some of these negative feelings were discussed earlier. Accommodation may be accompanied by negative attitudes of resentment and hostility, which can lead to conflict and sore feelings between family members. On the other hand, avoidance of conflict can cause excessive distance between family members. Conflict and excessive distancing are building blocks for family dysfunction.

Inappropriate shifts in responsibilities and roles of family members (such as excessive dependence on children to care for a parent with OCD) cause family dysfunction as well. For instance, Marilyn's husband was asked to remove the children from the home several evenings a week for several hours at a time while his wife performed her rituals without interruption. He felt resentment toward her, and the children were quite aware of his negative feelings. He would often become very angry and threaten to leave his wife, causing the children to fear he would abandon them. Though his behavior was accommodating, he harbored negative feelings—an important element of family dysfunction.

3. When family members decrease avoidance and decrease their involvement in accommodating behaviors, their loved ones do better in treatment.

Treatment requires that the person with OCD take risks. Risk taking means they will learn new ways to respond to the OCD fear messages that are different from their usual mode of reacting. They may set goals in treatment and take steps to change their patterns of reacting to OCD. Meanwhile, family members often continue their same pattern of reacting, and they unknowingly feed the OCD. Thus, when family members work concurrently with the person to decrease the feeding of OCD, the family is on common ground. Everyone is working on the same goals and on the same playing field. This collaborative process helps set the tone of fighting against the OCD symptoms instead of your loved one. In this way, ERP can be more effective.

At first, Cherry was reluctant to involve her husband and son in her ERP. She even put off telling them what they could do to help her take risks and fight her OCD. That meant giving up their help with checking things before leaving the house. Even harder was telling them to stop giving her reassurance. Until she felt stronger, they made an agreement. They would reassure Cherry once, then they were to answer with an agreed-upon response, such as, "For the sake of your health, I can't answer that question again." Her son, ever the comedian, sometimes answered, "For the sake of *my* health, I can't answer that question." Involving her family was a major part of Cherry's recovery process.

4. The family environment has an important impact on the person with OCD.

When family members express excessive criticism, hostility, or anger, it has a negative impact on the loved one with OCD. Emotional expressiveness includes excessive criticism and expressions of hostility and anger. Emotional expressiveness in these forms is associated with the relapse of symptoms. The more emotionally expressive the individual family members are (with hostility and critical remarks), the greater is the likelihood of a relapse of symptoms.

As already discussed, negative feelings can develop in families that accommodate OCD. Hostility leads to criticism and hurtful arguments. The person with OCD then feels greater frustration, shame, guilt, and other negative feelings that affect how they feel about themselves. These feelings can have a negative impact on motivation to change and commitment to the process of cognitive behavioral therapy. Treatment is difficult enough, and family support is an important factor in promoting treatment success.

Why Do Family Members Accommodate?

Before we discuss why family members accommodate, take a few moments to think about your own situation. Complete the Exploring Your Accommodation chart. Make copies for other family members to complete. You may want to discuss your answers.

Exploring Your Accommodation

Do you accommodate your loved one's OCD? In what way do you accommodate?

_____

_____

_____

_____

Why do you think you accommodate the OCD?

_____

_____

_____

_____

Describe your earliest memory of accommodating the OCD.

_____

_____

_____

Why did you decide to react to the OCD in this manner?

_____

_____

_____

_____

Family members suffer from tremendous conflict and confusion as OCD rears its ugly head within the home and family life. Normal, everyday situations become fertile territory for emotional outbursts, fear, temper tantrums, and arguments. It's natural to respond by trying hard to decrease this conflict and tension. Often, and quite unfortunately, your accommodating reactions to OCD symptoms do successfully decrease tension and conflict. In other words, they seem to work.

Accommodating behaviors can help your loved one function better in the short term. These behaviors can also help decrease tensions in the short term. Through the help of accommodations, perhaps your loved one can enjoy more activities day to day, get to school or work on time, or get through the day with less pain, distress, and chaos. The key idea here is short-term versus long-term relief. Over the long term, OCD grows on these feeding behaviors.

Family members also accommodate as they try to protect their loved one from OCD fears and threats. For instance, it's a basic instinct for parents to feel compelled to protect their children, and that includes protecting children from fears. How many of us as a child had a fear of monsters at bedtime, only to be comforted after Mom or Dad checked the closet and under our bed? Spouses and close friends often try to protect each other from pain and suffering, even going so far as to put their own lives in danger. In our courts, spouses are not required to testify against each other. We want to protect our family members from life's fears and negative events, and accommodations and reassurances seem to be natural responses to this instinct. Complete the Soothing Fears chart to explore how you soothe your own fears and the fears of others.

Soothing Fears

If you are a parent, outside of OCD fears, how have you tried to soothe your child's fears?

_____

_____

_____

_____

How were your fears soothed when you were a child?

_____

_____

_____

_____

How do you soothe your own fears as an adult?

_____

_____

_____

_____

As an adult, how have you soothed the fears of a loved one?

_____

_____

_____

_____

Family members also accommodate their loved one's OCD out of their own fears. Some families report that their loved one becomes more distressed or angry when the family refuses to accommodate. The family fears the anger and the negative reactions of the family member with OCD. They accommodate in order to avoid an angry outburst or an excessive negative reaction. Some family members are fearful of their own emotional reactions to their loved one's distress or anger. In an effort to quell their own emotions and anxiety, they jump in with the quick fix of accommodating, and all seems well until the next OCD episode. But beware! You are learning that accommodating reactions are often a short-term fix to a longer-term problem. It may work at first, but as the demands of OCD increase, you will have to make more and more of an effort to accommodate OCD in just the "right" way.

There is another negative effect that accommodating behaviors can have on your loved one's struggle with OCD. When you accommodate, you inadvertently send the message that it's okay, maybe even necessary, to do rituals in response to OCD's fear messages and threats. Your accommodations and your loved one's rituals pay too much respect to OCD. By stepping in to protect your loved one from OCD, you are modeling the belief that he or she cannot cope in other ways. You model the belief that your loved one needs to be protected and shielded from the fears. The message sent is that your loved one is too weak and too vulnerable to cope with the fears, the uncertainty, and the risk taking required to overpower and overcome OCD.

Summary

Family members can feel confused, guilty, fearful, angry, doubtful, disappointed, distraught, helpless, and hopeless. In an attempt to relieve these feelings, they can give in to the demands of OCD in whatever way works. Knowing they are feeding the OCD, they can be overwhelmed by even more feelings of guilt. Futile attempts to help can include participation in rituals, debating with the person with OCD, criticizing, and nagging. It's important to realize these are common feelings and common reactions to them. Acknowledging them will help you choose healthier, more supportive responses to your loved one's OCD.

Accommodation traps undermine the therapeutic goal of exposure and risk taking. They temporarily decrease the tension and conflict, helping your loved one function better in the short term. They don't, however, support long-term recovery. The next chapter introduces family contracting as a coping model. Coping will mean feeling the fear and facing the fear. Family contracting allows for a balance between encouraging your loved one and acknowledging the difficulties, while sending the message that you believe he or she can beat the OCD.

Chapter 5

The Need for Family Contracting

The previous chapter introduced you to the traps that people with OCD and their loved ones often face. Like other family members, you've been doing the best you can with the knowledge you had. You've accommodated and done things to reduce anxiety out of love for someone with OCD. Now the challenge will be learning new responses and implementing them. Some of these things will be hard to do, but you can do them for the same reason you did the accommodating: because of the love you have for the person. It is really an act of love to read this book and find out what you can do that will truly help your loved one.

The next step involves developing an understanding of the role you play during the intense OCD moments. While each family's OCD experiences are unique, there are similar threads that run through them. Many reactions to OCD situations are also similar, such as accommodating behaviors, negative feelings, and avoidance. Your goals will involve transforming OCD moments and your reactions to them.

Many family members repeatedly find themselves in the same challenging OCD situations, feeling guilt, remorse, confusion, or anger over how they handled their own emotions. Do you ever regret how you reacted toward your loved one with OCD? Do you wish that you could have a different relationship? Did you identify with the family members' experiences described in the previous chapter on accommodating? These are just some of the ways that family members can become involved and entrenched in the rituals of people with OCD. Countless families have shared in similar experiences.

FAMILY LIFE: THE REACTION CYCLE

The frustrating reaction cycle that has disrupted your family life does not have to continue. Your reaction to your loved one's obsessions and compulsions sets off his or her reactions to you and vice versa. Thus, a vicious cycle of interactions and patterns emerges.

The Reaction Cycle in Action

The No Contracting—No Risk Taking diagram that appears later in this chapter depicts a typical OCD moment with no contract in place. Later, in the Contracting and Risk Taking diagram, you'll see the difference that having a plan in place can make. For now, consider the Gonzalez family's story. Rita Gonzalez was feeling frustrated, confused, and helpless because she didn't know how to help her husband, José. OCD had moved in and taken out its wrath not only on José but on their relationship as well. José's uncertainty and obsessions about ordering and checking his possessions caused him to check his backpack repeatedly, making him late for class several days each week. Because of his OCD, he only took two classes at the community college and was having difficulty passing those classes.

On some days, José was able to get out of the door with just a few ritualistic checks, but on other days, he would seek reassurance and assistance from Rita in completing the checking ritual. Without a real understanding of how José's rituals and her accommodations worked to feed the OCD, Rita reacted in what appeared to be a logical manner. José seemed to need her help, and so she started assisting José in his checking rituals. On most occasions, after a couple rounds of accommodation and reassurance, José would experience relief from the anxiety and uncertainty. The checking ritual would end, and José was then able to leave for class. Unfortunately, both José and Rita had unknowingly traded long-term freedom from OCD for short-term relief from the OCD moment.

The Role of Learning in the Reaction Cycle

Now follow along with the cycle of interactions and patterns José and Rita had learned over time. José reacted to OCD by performing rituals. When the rituals seemingly took too long or "didn't work" (meaning he continued to experience the anxiety and uncertainty despite performing the rituals), José reacted by asking his wife for reassurance and assistance.

Note that reassurance seeking should be viewed as a type of ritual. It serves the same purpose. People with OCD seek reassurance to relieve the anxiety brought on by obsessions.

Rita reacted to José's requests by providing reassurance and accommodation of the checking ritual. Eventually, after several reassurances and accommodations, José felt better and was able to move on to class. It appeared as though the rituals and accommodations had worked! Maladaptive reactions such as rituals, reassurance, and accommodation, however, only serve to feed the OCD and make it stronger.

The Role of Reinforcement in the Reaction Cycle

It's important to understand how these reactions contribute to and perpetuate the reaction cycle. You can start with a basic term from behavioral theory called *reinforcement*. According to behavioral theory, behaviors and reactions are reinforced when followed by some thing or some event that the individual deems pleasurable or desirable. To illustrate this concept, imagine a boy named Johnny whose favorite treat is ice cream. For Johnny, ice cream is both pleasurable and desirable; it's better to have ice cream than to not have ice cream—it's reinforcing. Johnny and his mother make a deal. She agrees to give Johnny an ice cream cone each time he helps her out by walking the dog. When walking the dog (the behavior) is repeatedly followed by ice cream (the reinforcer or reward), the behavior is said to be *reinforced.*

For people with OCD, rituals and accommodation are often followed by relief from or a decrease in anxiety and uncertainty. Relief from the anxiety and uncertainty is a desirable outcome. After all, it seems better to *not* feel anxious than to feel anxious. When rituals and accommodations (the behaviors) are repeatedly followed by relief (the reinforcer), the rituals and accommodating behaviors are being reinforced by the reward of decreased anxiety and discomfort (or by the withdrawal of anxiety and discomfort).

José was reinforced for performing the rituals because the rituals seemingly rewarded him with relief from his anxiety. Rita was reinforced for providing reassurance and accommodation. She seemed to be rewarded for her accommodating behaviors when she experienced relief from observing José's anxiety, as well as relief from her own anxieties brought on by the OCD moment. After repeated interactions such as these, the reaction cycle becomes reinforcing for everyone (at least in the short term).

Reinforcement: Expecting More of the Same

The next concept related to the reinforcement of rituals and accommodation has to do with the effects these behaviors have on future situations. When a reaction or interaction is repeatedly reinforced, the result is an increased likelihood of reacting with the same behaviors the next time this or a similar situation arises. Looking at Johnny and the ice cream cones, he would probably continue saying yes when asked to walk the dog because he has been repeatedly reinforced with ice cream for complying with his mother's requests.

Now, apply this concept to José's and Rita's situation. Because José was repeatedly reinforced with relief from anxiety after performing rituals and requesting reassurance or accommodation, he was now all the more likely to rely on these maladaptive reactions the next time he was feeling anxious or uncertain. Rita continued providing reassurance and/or accommodation of the ritual when confronted with an OCD moment because these reactions seemed to work in the past. Without an understanding of the ways in which accommodation and reassurance feeds the OCD, José and Rita were unknowingly stuck perpetuating this vicious cycle of interactions. This cycle had them both reacting to OCD in ways that would make it grow bigger and stronger. In addition, each maladaptive reaction only served to increase the likelihood that these maladaptive reactions would continue.

Of course, family members do have an alternative to complying with requests for reassurance and accommodation. As the No Contracting—No Risk Taking diagram illustrates, family members can also make the decision to not comply with requests for reassurance or accommodation. This would occur on occasion with José and Rita. Sometimes out of frustration, impatience, or anger, Rita would refuse to accommodate his requests for reassurance or assistance with rituals. At other times, she simply refused because she realized that her assistance was not really helping to solve the problem.

When Rita did refuse his requests, José's anxiety would quickly grow, seemingly beyond his ability to cope. José would in turn react with either an outburst of anger or tears. Because there was no previously agreed-upon contract in place for managing these OCD moments, Rita was not prepared for how to respond. Out of desperation, she would often just give in and provide the reassurance and accommodations that he wanted. She could always hope for a different outcome the next time around. As a result, the OCD was made bigger and stronger. OCD continued to win!

CHANGING THE RULES

In José and Rita's cycle, sometimes Rita was able to withstand José's desperate pleas for reassurance and accommodation. Although this option was better because she didn't actively participate in feeding the OCD, her unexpected reaction still did not solve the problem. Her withholding of reassurance still had negative effects on José and his OCD. He often felt abandoned by Rita when she didn't help him with his rituals. After all, he had learned through her reinforcement that she would reassure and accommodate him in the midst of OCD moments. Why was this OCD moment any different? Why had the rules changed? Why wasn't she willing to help?

Now take another look at Johnny and the ice cream cones. Say that for the past two weeks, his mother had always given Johnny an ice cream cone in return for walking the dog, and then suddenly one day she changed the rules. What if, without consulting Johnny, she decided to not give him the ice cream cone in return for walking the dog? Imagine how Johnny would feel in this situation. How do you think he would feel about his mother? How do you think he might react toward her?

Apply this scenario to your own experiences with your loved one. You find yourself in a reoccurring OCD moment where your typical reaction is to provide reassurance or accommodation. As a result of past interactions, you have in fact taught your loved one to expect your reassurance and accommodation. In essence, the two of you have unknowingly developed a set of rules and expectations for reacting to each other during an OCD moment. Now suppose that, without prior discussion or agreement, you decide to no longer provide reassurance or accommodation. By making this decision in this manner, you disregard the rules and expectations that you and your loved one have developed. When you change the rules on your own, you leave yourself and your loved one unprepared for what will follow. Complete the Changing the Rules chart to explore how you have changed the rules in the midst of an OCD moment.

No Contracting—No Risk Taking

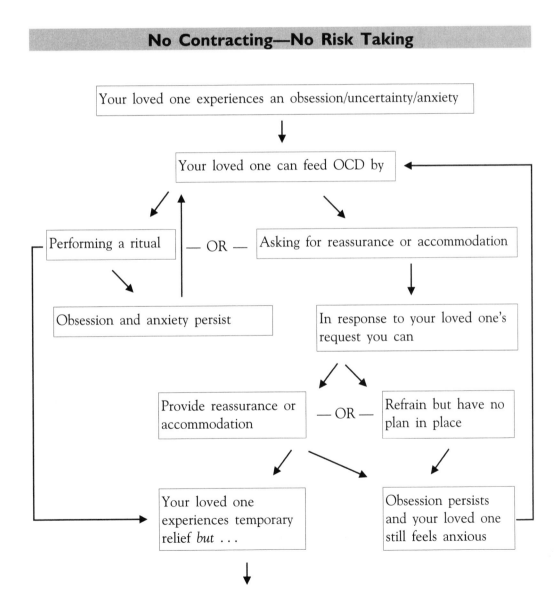

OCD is fed and made stronger!

Changing the Rules

Have you ever changed the rules for interacting with your loved one in the midst of an OCD moment? Describe the situation and describe how you think he or she felt in this situation.

_____

_____

_____

_____

What part of your loved one's reactions to this change caught you off guard? How did you react to your loved one?

_____

_____

_____

_____

Did your reactions support or interfere with recovery from OCD? What was the end result?

_____

_____

_____

_____

Why Going Cold Turkey Doesn't Work

Here is another point to consider when changing the rules unexpectedly. It might appear that withholding accommodation would lead to a successful outcome where OCD is not fed. But in most instances, that is not what happens. Abruptly changing the way things have been, or going cold turkey, doesn't usually bring about the desired outcome. Although you are not feeding the OCD with your reaction, your loved one is still suffering the anxiety and uncertainty of the obsession. In most cases, when reassurance and accommodation are not available, the person will just defer to another ritual that does not require your involvement. His or her own creativity often leads to developing an alternative version of the ritual. The end result remains the same—OCD is still fed and made bigger and stronger.

Taking Another Look

Look again at José and Rita's situation. Four weeks into his treatment, José and Rita took several steps forward in the process of José's recovery from OCD. They understood the roles of rituals, reassurance, and accommodation in feeding the OCD and making it stronger. They understood that there were alternatives to feeding the OCD when it was hungry. They understood that the longer they accommodated OCD and made it feel at home, the longer this unwelcome houseguest would stay. And most importantly, they both agreed to give the teamwork approach of contracting a fair try.

The Contract in Action

As you'll recall, José's obsessions and uncertainty caused him to check his backpack repeatedly each day before class. His rituals caused him to be late several days each week. On some of the more difficult days, José resorted to asking for reassurance and assistance with his checking ritual. Out of love, fear, or frustration, his wife Rita would usually comply and enter José's OCD world of rituals. As a result, the OCD was fed and made stronger, and the vicious cycle was strengthened.

The Contracting and Risk Taking diagram that follows demonstrates what changed as a result of the contracting process and practicing ERP. The OCD moment would start when José experienced an obsession about his backpack. "I'm not sure that I have everything I need in my backpack. What if I don't? What if I forgot something and I need it later?" José's first instinct was to react to the uncertainty and anxiety with a ritual. After all, that's the reaction that had been reinforced in the past. But then he'd remember that he had a choice. He could choose to feed the hungry OCD in an effort to get relief in the short term, or he could choose to abide by the contract and engage in ERP instead. He knew that if he chose ERP he might feel more anxious in the short term, but at least he'd be helping to make himself stronger as he starved the OCD and made it weaker. Rather than seek short-term relief, he opted for long-term freedom from OCD. And because of the planning involved when he and Rita developed the contract, José knew he could ask for her help in resisting the OCD. He decided it was time to show OCD who was in charge. It was time to kick this unwelcome houseguest out of their lives for good!

At first, José tried to resist the urge to check his backpack on his own. He was able to do this for a few minutes, but the OCD kept "upping the ante." The OCD didn't like that it wasn't being fed. OCD reacted by turning up the volume and putting even more pressure on José. The "what-if?" thoughts came in faster and louder. José experienced OCD's pressure as an increase in anxiety and an increase in the urge to check. He desperately wanted to give in to the quick fix of the ritual, but he reminded himself that if he held out long enough the OCD would give up and he would win.

As OCD continued to put more and more pressure on José, he had the option of bringing in the reinforcements. He could call for Rita's help. Now it was two against one. Just as they had agreed upon in the contract, Rita would step in and join José in the battle against OCD. Instead of asking Rita for reassurance or for help in checking his backpack, he'd ask for her help in resisting the urge to check so that he could defeat OCD. Together they would gang up on the OCD. Often, they played a verbal game against the OCD. José would start with, "You're just an annoying pain in the butt, OCD, telling me that I have to check my backpack or else . . . Maybe I don't have everything I need in my backpack, and maybe I do. But I can live without knowing that right now. So just shut up OCD!"

Then Rita would add, "Besides, José will deal with the situation, even if he finds out later that he doesn't have everything he needs. But he doesn't have to figure that out now. He'll deal with that possibility if and when it happens, but you're not getting your way this time, OCD! José is in charge!" After several more minutes of fighting with OCD, the uncertainty and anxiety would disappear, and the urge to check would pass. The Contracting and Risk Taking diagram depicts the options in a typical OCD moment when a contract is in place. You can see the obvious rewards of contracting for you and your loved one.

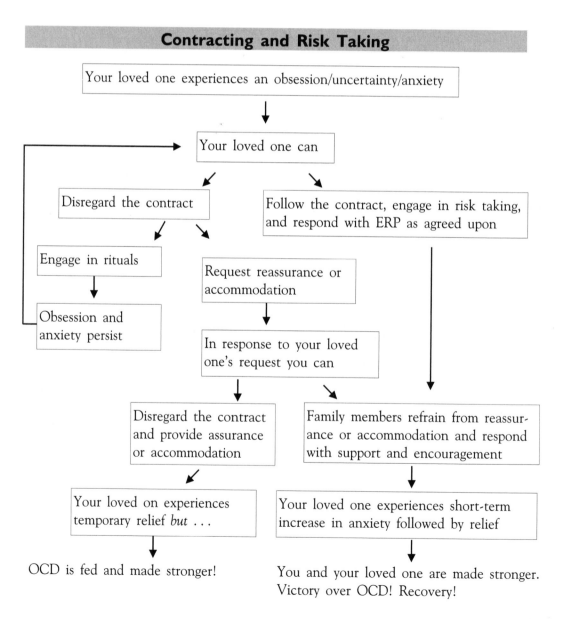

THE ROLE OF REINFORCEMENT IN UNLEARNING THE REACTION CYCLE

Now review what José and Rita learned from applying the contracting process. This chapter has already discussed the role of reinforcement in the development of the reaction cycle between your loved one, yourself, and the OCD. Reinforcement plays an equally important role within the process of ERP and contracting. Reinforcement helps everyone learn therapeutic and supportive responses that encourage risk taking and recovery. It aids in the "unlearning" of the unhealthy reaction cycle as well. The very process that led you into this situation is the same process that will lead you out. Again, consider two important principles of behavioral theory:

1. Behaviors and reactions are reinforced when followed by some thing or some event that the individual deems pleasurable or desirable.

If you apply this principle to José and Rita's experience with the contracting process, José was reinforced for *not* performing the ritual. He held out and resisted the ritual, and eventually he was rewarded with relief from his uncertainty and anxiety. He learned that even if he does nothing to neutralize the anxiety—that if he just waits it out—it will go away on its own.

Rita was also reinforced for providing José with support and for encouraging ERP and risk taking. She was able to support José in the OCD moment, and he was able to remain in the OCD situation without performing a ritual. In turn, Rita was rewarded with witnessing his triumph over OCD and experiencing relief from her own anxieties brought on by the OCD moment.

After repeated interactions and planned-out responses to OCD moments, these new responses to each other and to OCD were reinforced and strengthened. At the same time, the old reactions that fed the vicious cycle of OCD reactions were "unlearned." The end result was a new way of responding to OCD and each other that weakened OCD while strengthening the family.

2. When a reaction or interaction is repeatedly reinforced, the result is an increased likelihood of reacting with the same behaviors the next time this or a similar situation arises.

After repeated use of ERP, as agreed upon in the contracting process, José was more likely to rely on ERP and risk taking (rather than rituals, reassurance, or accommodation) the next time he was confronted with a similar situation. Rita continued in her contracted role of providing encouragement of ERP because this response worked the last few times.

When José and Rita had a firm understanding of the ways in which rituals, accommodation, and reassurance fed the OCD, they could knowingly make different and therapeutic choices within the OCD moment. They were no longer stuck perpetuating this vicious cycle of interactions. They responded in ways that would support and strengthen each other. Together, they weakened the OCD and returned it to an insignificant place in their lives.

You can see how contracting was helpful for José and Rita. The chapters ahead will continue discussing contracting as a means of problem solving for your family. You will go through the process of contracting and responding differently. Through contracting and a strategic stance against the OCD, you can work with your loved one to end the reaction cycle you are experiencing as a result of OCD.

Summary

You may find yourself repeatedly facing the same challenging OCD situations and then feeling guilt, regret, frustration, and anger about how you responded. If you've become entrenched in your loved one's rituals, you're not alone. You're now beginning to understand the role of rituals, reassurance, and accommodations in feeding the OCD and making it stronger.

Reinforcement plays an important role in the development of the reaction cycle between your loved one, yourself, and the OCD. When reassurance and participation in rituals works to relieve anxiety the first time, these reactions are reinforced and you try them the next time you're confronted with a similar situation. It also plays an important role in recovery. Through the contracting process, you can use reinforcement to help you "unlearn" unhealthy reactions to OCD.

Chapter 6

Contracting, the Solution for Family Problem Solving

Interrupting the reaction cycle requires that you respond differently. You'll identify new ways of responding to your loved one's OCD in a helpful, therapeutic manner. Notice that we use the word *responding*. In this chapter, we'll describe the differences between reacting and responding to OCD moments. Don't expect change overnight from yourself or your loved one. Your family's way of relating and responding to OCD developed gradually, and it will change gradually. Just as you can't expect your loved one to always resist rituals, you can't expect yourself to respond in a perfect way, either. Congratulate yourself for improvement, and don't expect perfection.

OCD: THE PREDICTABLE SITUATIONS

Some OCD situations cannot be predicted, and they catch you off guard and unprepared. But oftentimes, OCD situations become very predictable as they occur over and over again. For instance, Marilyn's husband described the decontamination ritual the family endured every morning at breakfast. She wiped clean the cereal box, bowls, and spoons as well as the cabinets and drawers where they were stored. After her cleaning rituals, she would repeatedly ask him for reassurance that everything was "clean enough." This occurred every day before breakfast. Her rituals could take as long as forty-five minutes to complete and sometimes made him late for work. Needless to say, tensions were high and arguments were common on those days. This OCD situation was predictable, difficult, and frustrating for everyone involved. Describe predictable situations that occur repeatedly in your family in the Predictable OCD Situations chart.

Predictable OCD Situations

Describe a few of the repetitive or predictable situations in which you and your loved one with OCD sometimes find yourselves.

1. _____

_____

2. _____

_____

3. _____

_____

You're All in This Together

The whole family often gets stuck in the traps of OCD. Luckily, your loved one's recovery from OCD can also include you and your own behavioral changes. This means you can actively participate and thus have some sense of control in the treatment process. The use of contracting involves your recovery from OCD as well. You have become intertwined in this powerful and painful illness. OCD is also causing distress and heartache for you.

You and your loved one share many common feelings and experiences as a result of OCD entering your lives. There are many common threads between your reaction to OCD and his or her reaction to OCD. Recognizing the emotions and reactions that you share can help you to better understand each other in your shared struggle with OCD. You both react to OCD. You both likely feel "stuck" in the way you respond to difficult OCD moments. Your loved one is stuck reacting to OCD with rituals. He or she listens to fear messages and checks, washes, organizes, or performs some other ritual. You are stuck reacting to OCD with accommodating behaviors. You likely debate, reassure, participate, observe, or avoid something in reaction to OCD. You each experience a change in the intensity of feelings about the OCD moment after it passes, whether feeling positive or negative. You may feel relieved, more distressed, or both.

Both your accommodating behaviors and your loved one's rituals are aimed at reducing anxiety and distress *in the moment*. However, neither reaction ever really solves the problem of OCD. Although it seems that you are addressing the situation at hand, it's likely that another similar OCD moment is right around the corner. The longer you both rely on the same frustrating and ineffective reactions to OCD, the greater your struggles with OCD will grow. To recover, your loved one must learn to cope with the anxiety of OCD moments without relying upon rituals. To recover, you must learn to live with your own anxiety about the OCD moment without relying upon accommodating behaviors. Both rituals and accommodating behaviors are reactions that only strengthen the OCD.

Contracting can lead you on the road to freedom and toward recovery for the family as a whole. Understanding how to be supportive in a therapeutic way can help you feel more hopeful and make more effective decisions during OCD moments. Your responses can deflect your distress and help you feel more empowered with your loved one. OCD does not have to overpower and rewrite the rules for the family.

Because of the many similarities between accommodating behaviors and rituals, you can think of accommodating behaviors as "pseudorituals." Pseudorituals serve you in the same way that rituals serve your loved one. Just as rituals serve to ward off some distressing emotion or feared outcome, you rely on pseudorituals to avoid your own distressing emotions or feared outcomes. Complete the Exploring Your Avoidance chart. You may want to make copies for other family members and discuss your answers.

Exploring Your Avoidance

When you engage in pseudorituals of accommodation, what uncomfortable feelings, situations, or feared outcomes are you avoiding?

1. _____

_____

2. _____

_____

3. _____

_____

COLLABORATING ON CONTRACTS

Let's discuss more closely the contracting process. Contracts involve an agreement on a matter between at least two parties. Agreements involving how to respond to OCD moments are called *behavioral contracts*. With the contracting process, you want to see eye to eye so that the family and the person with OCD agree that something needs to change. In this way, you can negotiate fair and reasonable contracts. Everyone needs to have a say in the process. It's important for you to understand how hard it will be for your loved one to change and respond differently to the OCD. He or she also needs to know how difficult it will be for you to respond differently to the OCD.

Since you want to be on the same page, it will be helpful for the entire family to read this book, including the person with OCD. All of you will then have similar information and a strategy to help you communicate more effectively. This workbook serves as a foundation for developing a more effective means of communication. You can continue to refer to the workbook's themes and issues as needed during the contracting process. This book is designed to help you through each step of the way.

Contracting is an important strategy in your loved one's and your recovery from OCD. In order for contracting to be most effective, it must be mutually agreed upon and involve the collaboration of other family members. The team approach of the contracting engages you in the process of creating specific plans and realistic expectations for everyone involved. The contract will help you plan the details for managing specific situations made difficult by OCD. If you devise a contract and proactive plan of action without your loved one's participation, knowledge, or motivation, then you will most likely experience difficulty carrying it out as planned. It takes both of you to make the contract work. Chapter 11 will discuss how you can help if your loved one is refusing treatment.

Proactive Problem Solving

By planning ahead for OCD moments, contracting is designed to engage you and your loved one in a proactive process of problem solving. Creating a contract will also change your style of communication or your lack of communication. You will design your contracts to directly confront specific situations resulting from OCD's demands.

This strategy provides an alternative to the typical ways families react to OCD moments. Contracting allows you to clearly redefine how to be supportive. It creates the opportunity for you to *respond* to moments made difficult by OCD rather than just *react* to these moments. What's the difference between responding and reacting? Responding involves a preplanned and well-thought-out approach that is based on a strategy and a philosophy. Responding allows everyone to feel more in control while working together, and it supports the team approach to achieving the long-term goals of ERP. In contrast, reacting to OCD is often impulsive and feels out of control. Reacting usually results in everyone feeling badly, while interfering with your and your loved one's long-term goals of gaining freedom from OCD.

Linda's mother reacted to OCD's demands on her daughter and felt frustrated, confused, and helpless. She cleaned Linda's bedroom and bathroom daily to remove all possible contamination for her. It helped in the short run. But the cleaning ritual became more elaborate, and eventually Linda wanted her mother to clean the bathroom before each shower. Helping with the cleaning was a short-term quick fix. Contracting helped Linda and her mother work as a team to decide how to respond more therapeutically to the OCD demands.

Emotional Decision Making: You Feel . . . and Then You React

One advantage of this planned team approach is that it helps to avoid the emotional reasoning that occurs during challenging and intense OCD moments. Emotional reasoning is different from reasoning based on logic and sound judgment. Reasoning based solely on emotions can lead to poor decisions and the use of poor judgment. This type of reasoning occurs when tensions are high and everyone is feeling overwhelmed in the moment. Emotional reasoning interferes with effective decision making because it's more difficult to think clearly when we're upset or overwhelmed. Feeling overwhelmed, you base decisions on intense feelings or the desire to avoid negative feelings, rather than a rational thought process and clear mind.

Emotional reasoning is a main component of reacting rather than responding to situations, and often occurs when you're trying to solve a problem or make a decision during an intense OCD moment. This often results in an emotional reaction instead of a strategic and supportive response. The core problem is that we cannot depend on ourselves to be logical and rational when we're feeling upset or overwhelmed. When we use emotional reasoning as a basis for solving problems, we often react in ways that are poorly thought out and sometimes hurtful. Oftentimes, in the intensity of the moment, we don't even consider the consequences of our emotionally based reactions until it's too late.

Stan Parks reported a situation made more difficult by his own emotional reasoning during difficult OCD moments. His brother Gene would call him on the phone, unable to make simple decisions. He'd sometimes call Stan at work, anxious and crying; at times he seemed emotionally paralyzed. Stan would become more and more upset as he listened to his brother's anguish. Out of guilt and desperation, he made more and more decisions for Gene, including such trivial daily decisions as what to eat, when to go to sleep, and which clothes he should wear.

Stan became more and more overloaded with the responsibility of Gene's daily decisions and felt even more scared and guilty for accommodating the OCD. He knew that taking over Gene's choices probably made Gene feel even more scared and dependent on him for the answers. He felt that he was making the OCD into a bigger problem than it was already. But Stan was trying to make both of them feel better and to alleviate Gene's guilt of the moment by helping Gene with a few simple decisions. Stan acknowledged the unanticipated consequences of accommodating Gene.

Quick Fixes—The Path of Least Resistance

In an effort to manage and move past the situation at hand, like Stan, you may find yourself choosing what appears to be the path of least resistance. You're doing whatever you do to end a difficult OCD situation and frustration as quickly as possible so that you can continue on through your day. Does this sound familiar? Explore how emotional thinking affects your problem solving by completing the Emotional Reasoning chart.

Emotional Reasoning

Describe some situations when you used emotional reasoning to solve a problem.

1. _____

_____

2. _____

_____

3. _____

_____

Does emotional reasoning seem to contribute to immediate relief of problems?

_____

_____

Does emotional reasoning seem to contribute to long-term solutions? Do the problems reoccur? _____

_____

The most immediate solution to a difficult situation is often based on emotional reasoning, and efforts result in a quick fix. Such solutions certainly can help the family continue on with daily life, but giving in to the enticing lure of a quick fix is just another trap into which OCD hopes you will fall. Remember that OCD grows when you feed it. Emotional reasoning will lead you down the path of least resistance when quick fixes are used to cope with OCD moments. You are catering to OCD's demands and making it more comfortable. You are feeding the OCD filet mignon! The result: OCD grows and becomes stronger.

Linda's mother was providing quick fixes when she cleaned her daughter's bedroom and bathroom, agreeing to more and more elaborate cleaning rituals. Stan provided quick fixes every time he made a decision for Gene. Quick fixes feed OCD. They send the message that the OCD behavior is necessary and important. This only validates and reinforces the need for checking, cleaning, and reassurance rituals. See the "Quick Fix" diagram for how quick fixes develop.

The path of least resistance can also lead to quick fixes that feed your own anger and frustration. These feelings of anger and frustration can lead you to accommodate the rituals in an effort to lessen the sting of OCD. You may feel that you just want to get through a tough moment and seek relief from your loved one's state of distress. Likewise, your feelings of anger and frustration may lead you to avoid situations that may trigger your loved one's obsessions. Solutions such as these only serve to strengthen the hold that OCD has on your lives. List your own quick fixes in the chart following the diagram.

Wishing for Change Overnight

You may relate to what you're reading here but feel hesitant to introduce new ways of responding into the family. You may be asking yourself, "How will my loved one react?" Life may already feel hard enough at home, and you may not feel strong enough to introduce more struggles. You should know that contracting is not an all-or-nothing approach. Contracting does not require that you, as the support person, abruptly eliminate all of your accommodating behaviors at once. Although accommodating behaviors prove to be frustrating for you, they have also served a function in your relationship. They have sometimes given you short-term relief or a reprieve from distress and other negative feelings.

Because your pseudorituals (accommodating behaviors) work to some degree in the short run, you cannot realistically expect yourself to successfully make necessary

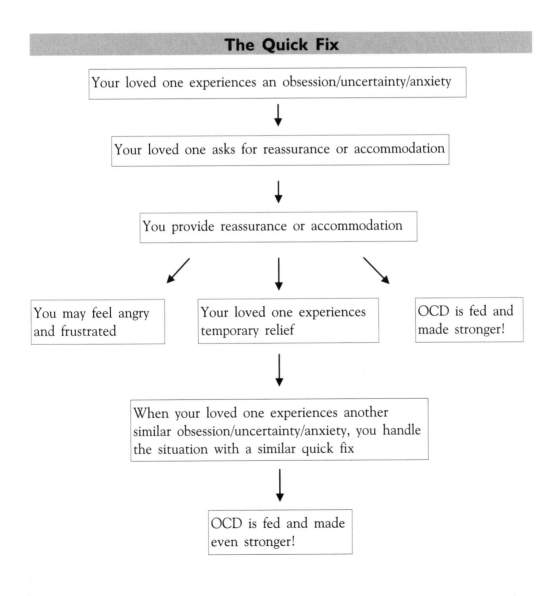

changes overnight, any more than you would expect your loved one to eliminate OCD rituals overnight. It took you both quite a while to get to where you are today, and continued patience will help you find your way back together. Your path toward recovery will include taking small steps in the right direction rather than perpetuating negative steps in the wrong direction. The required changes are often difficult, even terrifying, for everyone involved. You are all giving up some form of short-term comfort or quick fix for the long-term freedom from the grip of OCD.

Your Quick Fixes

What short-term quick fixes do you find yourself relying on in difficult situations?

1. _____

_____

2. _____

_____

3. _____

_____

Do these quick fixes get you the short-term results you want? How about long-term results?

_____

_____

_____

_____

The cooperative spirit of contracting is maximized when all family members become involved, including the person with OCD, and you agree together that it's best to begin to cease participation in rituals and accommodating behaviors. You need to agree together that it's time to slow the feeding of the OCD, put the OCD on a diet, restricting and setting limits on OCD's demands.

GENERAL PROBLEM SOLVING IN RELATIONSHIPS

The contracting process follows the process of everyday problem solving in relationships. Problem solving, whether or not related to OCD, involves taking a series of steps. You probably make decisions and solve problems all the time without really thinking formally about the actual steps of the thought process. But examining these steps can help you better understand the foundation for finding solutions for OCD problems within the process of contracting. Here are the steps you would take:

1. **Share perspectives.** Conflict can often arise when two people don't agree or have the same perspective. You may have different angles on the same issue, so you view the problem in different ways. You might have different goals on how you want a situation to work out. Your ideas may differ. People can have intense feelings about their individual perspectives, and that can make it harder to solve the problem. Contracting offers you the opportunity to share your different points of view as you discuss the problematic situations that occur in OCD moments. It offers an opportunity to face the problems rather than avoid them or feel angry and upset about how the problems are handled in the moment. Contracting also offers a way to work together to find solutions that you can all try to live with.

2. **Choose a calm moment.** Problem solving is most effective when you're calm. As discussed, emotional reasoning and strong emotions can interfere with thinking and making good choices. It's important to find a calm time to discuss problems and to avoid discussions in the OCD moment or close to the OCD moment. Calmness means that arguing has ceased, and the hostility or tears are over for the time being.

3. **Define the problem area and desired outcome.** When you're calm, you then need to describe the problem area and define it clearly. It may be that you each have a different idea of the problem area, and it's important to recognize this discrepancy. Problem solving will be more productive when you both know exactly what problem you're working on at the moment. Make certain you look at the problem from each of your perspectives. You might even write out the problem as it has been defined from each of your perspectives. Problems can be large and complex. When defining the problem area, it's important to break down the problem into smaller, more manageable parts. Then you can deal with each part of the problem, one step at a time.

4. **Brainstorm ideas for a solution.** After defining a problem area, think about how you want the situation to change. What is the outcome you are hoping for? What is your goal? When problem solving with others, ask about their thoughts and desired outcomes or goals. Now it's time to brainstorm for all kinds of solutions. The ideas may not be perfect answers, but write a list of solutions anyway. One poor or silly solution may lead to a better solution if you let yourself think over all the different ideas. Brainstorming options is a time for collaborating, not blaming or defending yourself for past or current choices. You will need to work hard to stay focused on a solution, rather than argue about the accuracy of everyone's perspectives.

5. **Evaluate ideas.** Now it's time to take your brainstorming to the next level. Think about the pros and cons of each solution, or option, and the possible

outcomes. The questions may be, "How might this solution turn out if we use it to solve the problem? What may happen if we choose this option? Will we achieve what we need? How might this option impact on others?" These are the kinds of questions that can allow you to think out solutions to a problem and find the answer that works best for you.

When problem solving on your own, remember that listening to your own thoughts and concerns is important. When problem solving with others, remember to listen carefully to the other people involved as well. You can let them know you are listening through your body language, by making eye contact and looking at them without reacting negatively (frowning, rolling your eyes, sighing heavily). It's often helpful to restate other people's ideas and perspectives after they've finished speaking. In this way, you can ensure that you have heard the other person correctly and understand fully what he or she has said to you.

6. **Choose one option.** In the end, you need to choose one of the options that came up in brainstorming. It's important to choose a solution that you feel ready and committed to carry out. If you think you may not follow through or might feel angry and resentful, then this may not be the best solution. If all of you compromise and work toward getting everyone's needs met to some degree, there is a higher likelihood of success. The solution that you choose should be written in specific and behavioral terms so that everyone knows exactly how to implement the solution.

7. **Implement your idea and evaluate the results.** Follow through on the chosen solution and see how it works for you. Evaluate the outcome by answering the following questions: Did this solution solve the problem? Is this solution working for you? If not, did you think of the disadvantages of this option before you tried it (when you thought about the pros, cons, and possible outcomes)? How would you solve the problem differently in the future?

8. **Invite a third party (optional).** With OCD situations, it can be helpful to have a behavior therapist or objective outside person help you negotiate a solution. A third party can help you slow down and communicate your thoughts about the problem area so that you can define and clarify the problem, work through the steps of brainstorming, and evaluate different options. A third party can help you find a meeting ground, work out a plan that addresses everyone's needs, and oversee the implementation of the solution to the problem.

Practice Strategies for Problem Solving

You can use the Brainstorming Worksheet and Idea Evaluation Worksheet to aid you in problem solving. They will help walk you through the steps just discussed. Before reading the next chapter on implementing contracting for OCD, try out this kind of systematic problem solving. Experiment with some everyday problems that are unrelated to OCD and see how it works for you. Make extra copies of the worksheets so you can get a lot of practice at solving problems and communicating in this manner.

Brainstorming Worksheet

The problem from your perspective: _____

_____

_____

The problem from the other people's perspective: _____

_____

_____

The desired goal or outcome, from your perspective: _____

_____

_____

The desired goal or outcome, from the other person's perspective: _____

_____

_____

Brainstorm possible solutions:

Idea A: _____

_____

_____

Idea B: _____

_____

_____

Idea C: _____

_____

_____

Idea D: _____

_____

_____

Idea Evaluation Worksheet

Use the following questions to discover the pros, cons, and possible outcomes for each idea:

a. How might this solution turn out if you use it to solve the problem?

b. What may happen if you choose this option?

c. Will you achieve what you need?

d. How might this option impact others?

	Pros	Cons	Possible Outcomes
Idea A			
Idea B			
Idea C			
Idea D			

Choose one option as the solution and try it out. _____

Did this solution solve the problem? _____

Is this solution working for everyone? _____

If not, had you thought of the disadvantages of this option before you tried it (when you had thought about the pros, cons, and possible outcomes)? _____

How would you solve the problem differently in the future? _____

_____

_____

_____

Summary

Contracting will help you respond differently to OCD moments, as you interrupt the reaction cycle. Your entire family has gotten stuck in the traps of OCD, and every family member needs to play a role in escaping these traps. Encourage each of your family members, including the person with OCD, to read this book. This will help you each understand how contracting will lead your family toward recovery. Working as a team, you'll be able to apply problem-solving principles to OCD situations, instead of using quick fixes that only solve the immediate problem and ultimately feed the OCD.

Chapter 7

Creating the Family Contract

As you've discovered more about your loved one's OCD and how family members ommonly react to OCD situations, you may have seen yourself in some of the situations described in this book. You've hopefully gained insight into your own temporary problem-solving strategies or quick fixes. Now it's time to put this knowledge to work and move forward, using behavioral contracts as a tool for responding differently to OCD and freeing yourself from the grips of OCD.

IDENTIFY THE PROBLEM AREAS

You'll first need to identify the day-to-day areas or situations that are made more difficult because of OCD. Take some time to refer back to the situations that came to mind as you read the previous chapter and review the answers you provided about your own accommodating behaviors. The questions were designed to help you address your own needs, as well as the needs of your family. Complete the Impact of OCD chart to gain further perspective on the impact of OCD on your life. Make copies for other family members.

Impact of OCD

In what ways does your loved one's OCD have an impact on you?

In what ways do you participate in your loved one's rituals?

_____

_____

Describe one reoccurring situation where you participate in your loved one's rituals.

_____

_____

In what ways do you assist your loved one in avoiding situations, people, or things?

_____

_____

Describe one type of situation where you repeatedly assist in your loved one's avoidance. _____

_____

What responsibilities do you repeatedly take on because of your loved one's rituals or avoidance? _____

_____

Describe one situation where you repeatedly take on your loved one's responsibilities.

_____

_____

Describe how your loved one's responsibilities have decreased as a result of OCD rituals and avoidance. _____

_____

Describe how your loved one's rituals and avoidance increase your own daily responsibilities. _____

_____

How have expectations for your loved one's role and responsibilities changed within the family as a direct result of OCD?

_____

_____

COMMON DIFFICULT SITUATIONS

Families often report that their daily routine is made more difficult as a result of their loved one's OCD. Because of the frustrations and interference of OCD, family members frequently anticipate certain activities or situations with great caution or dread. The following list gives examples of activities and situations in which many families report having difficulties. List the reoccurring activities and situations that are made more difficult for your family because of your loved one's OCD on the Difficult Situations chart that follows.

- Self-care activities, such as showering, using the toilet, getting dressed, brushing teeth, making the bed, daily grooming, and hair care
- Leaving the house on time for important events, such as work, school, or social commitments
- Getting in or out of the car
- Having guests over to the home
- Eating meals together
- Participating in household chores, such as taking out the trash, washing dishes, dusting, or vacuuming
- Driving
- Being affectionate with others
- Sharing belongings with family members
- Adapting to changes in the typical routine
- Paying bills
- Shopping (making decisions)

Difficult Situations

List the reoccurring activities and situations that are made more difficult due to your loved one's OCD.

1. _____

2. _____

3. _____

4. _____

5. _____

6. _____

7. _____

8. _____

ASSESSMENT OF ACCOMMODATING BEHAVIORS

Now that you are more aware of the daily problem areas, you are ready to begin assessing the accommodating behaviors in your family. These differ not only from one family to another, but they also differ within each family. Self-monitoring will help your family members increase their awareness of their own roles in the OCD situations.

You will be using several methods for monitoring your accommodating behaviors over the next few weeks. During step 1, you will record the frequency of your accommodating behaviors. This will help you recognize the extent to which you participate in OCD situations. During step 2, you will provide more details and record a brief description of each situation leading up to an accommodation. During step 3, you will acknowledge and identify the feelings you experience as a result of accommodating your loved one's OCD. Each step will help you gain a deeper understanding of your role in OCD situations and identify areas for change.

Step 1

Are you aware of how often you accommodate your loved one's OCD? To determine the frequency, you will need to pay close attention and make a record of each occurrence. As you increase your awareness of your accommodating behaviors, you may even begin to notice more subtle behaviors that you were not aware of previously. During the next four days, record the number of times per day that you engage in accommodating behavior on the Frequency of Accommodating Behaviors chart. Make copies of the chart so that you can repeat this exercise. Each day, place a mark in the second column every time you engage in an accommodating behavior. Write the total number of times you engaged in accommodating behavior each day in the third column.

Frequency of Accommodating Behaviors

Day	Engaged in Accommodating Behavior	Total

Step 2

The Frequency of Accommodating Behaviors chart increases your awareness of your role in your loved one's OCD. Step 2 requires that you pay close attention to the types of accommodating behaviors and to the exact situations that tend to cause them. Over the next four days, list the different OCD situations in which you react with an accommodating behavior on the Accommodating Behavior Log. Make copies of the log, so you can repeat this exercise.

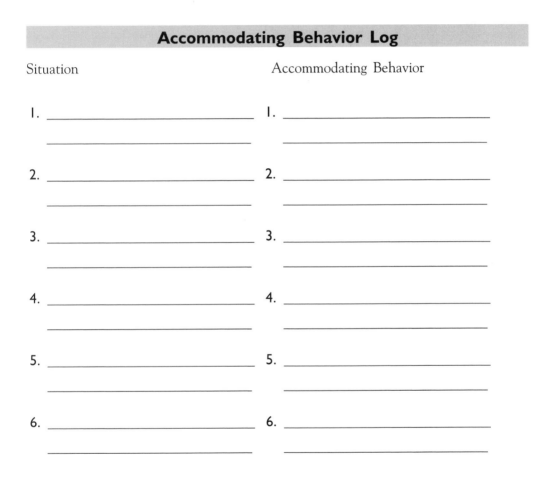

Accommodating Behavior Log

Situation	Accommodating Behavior
1. _____	1. _____
2. _____	2. _____
3. _____	3. _____
4. _____	4. _____
5. _____	5. _____
6. _____	6. _____

Step 3

You should be getting a clearer picture of the daily activities and situations that are made more difficult by OCD and by accommodating reactions. Over the next four days, use the Feelings Diary that follows to become more aware of the emotional impact of OCD.

There are two main components to this diary, and each is important for freeing yourself and your loved one from the grips of OCD. The first part requires that you monitor the feelings you experience as a result of accommodating OCD. Review the feelings discussed in chapter 4 to help you differentiate how you are feeling in each OCD situation. Each day, check off the feelings you experience. The second part requires you to think about how these feelings may be impacting your relationship. At the end of the four days, list the feelings you've checked the most often. Using a scale of 1 to 100 (with 100 being most hurtful or helpful), gauge how hurtful or helpful these feelings may be to your relationship. Do these situations result in emotions that bring you and your loved one together in the fight against OCD, or are they creating tension and distance between you and your loved one? Remember that OCD is the enemy here. You and your loved must work hard to team up against OCD and not work against each other.

FEELINGS DIARY

Feelings Experienced	Day			
Situation—Accommodating Behavior				
Distressed				
Angry				
Resentful				
Despairing				
Frustrated				
Confused				
Helpless				
Overwhelmed				
Doubtful				
Happy				
Satisfied				
Guilty				
Disappointed				
Sad				
Worried				

The feelings you've checked the most often:	How much are these feelings helpful or hurtful to your relationship? Use a scale of 1 to 100:	
	Helpful	**Hurtful**
1. _____	_____	_____
2. _____	_____	_____
3. _____	_____	_____
4. _____	_____	_____
5. _____	_____	_____
6. _____	_____	_____

Through monitoring your accommodating behavior and reactions to OCD situations, you have learned more about yourself and your interactions with your loved one. Perhaps you've recognized a tendency to be excessively vigilant in an effort to protect your loved one from difficult OCD situations, triggers, and symptoms. You may have tried to avoid potentially difficult OCD situations or to protect yourself from the full impact of OCD. Regardless of the reason for your vigilance, it likely serves in an effort to reduce high levels of stress and chronic chaos, which often run rampant in households affected by OCD. Through self-monitoring, you are starting to harness this vigilance in a helpful way. You can now use your increased awareness to identify important goals and problem areas to be addressed.

By charting your feelings, you have become more aware of your own emotions and how they impact your reaction to each OCD situation. This will make it easier to assess areas that require attention and change. You have also become more aware of how these feelings impact your relationship.

IDENTIFY GOALS

You now have a list of problem areas to address. In order to take action, you and your loved one will need to choose the first area you want to affect. You may want to review your completed Accommodating Behavior Log together. It will help you identify a specific situation or area for change. By discussing the problem areas in this way, you will be in a position to identify and agree upon goals together.

It's important that you negotiate and agree upon what you want to address. There are usually a number of situations that are problematic, so if you find yourselves stuck and unable to agree on certain areas, move on to something of mutual concern. You will need to agree upon the order in which problem situations will be addressed through contracting. This will often depend on where those related exposure exercises fall on your loved one's hierarchy (i.e. graduated list of anxiety-provoking situations).

Once you've agreed upon a problem area for contracting, identify and define the long-term goal related to that problem. In other words, how do you want that situation to be different for both yourself and your loved one? What types of behaviors and reactions will no longer occur once the goal has been achieved? How will behaviors and reactions change once the goal has been achieved? It's important to keep in mind that goals should be realistic and concrete, with very small challenges at first. Long-term goals that are too large or unrealistic will likely be abandoned as frustration mounts and motivation vanishes during those difficult OCD moments.

Successful contracting around a single problem area and long-term goal often involves several separate steps of increasingly difficult exposure for the individual with OCD. Consequently, these problem areas and long-term goals may need to be further broken down into smaller steps and short-term goals. Keep in mind that your short-term goals will involve related exposure and ritual prevention steps for the person with OCD. Whenever possible, try to coordinate goals with ERP exercises your loved one is working on.

Create Short-Term Goals

Just how are long-term goals broken into short-term goals? Together with the person with OCD, you can identify smaller steps that you can take in the direction of your long-term goal. Arrange these short-term goals in order of increasingly difficult exposure. To do this, ask your loved one to assign a number from 1 to 100 to each short-term goal, according to the perceived anxiety level (on this scale, 100 is the highest level of anxiety). This helps everyone understand the degree of anxiety surrounding a particular solution or response option.

Identify short-term goals in specific terms. Once you define the necessary short-term goals, you will both have a clearer idea of the approximate time line for achieving these goals. Target dates for long-term goals as well as short-term goals help keep the focus on the future and change. Target dates provide a basis for comparing actual change to your agreed-upon planned expectations for change.

Now that you have a better understanding of your role in your loved one's OCD, you are in a position to plan ahead and respond in ways that are supportive of shared goals. You will need to brainstorm options for responding differently and avoiding feeding the OCD. You can include your loved one in this process as long as your loved one's requests are reasonable. Throughout the brainstorming process, be sure to consider the pros, cons, and potential consequences of each alternative response. Ask yourself whether the alternative response is reasonable and be sure that it does not inadvertently feed the OCD. Use the OCD Feeding Chart to help you evaluate your options.

Some of your goals may involve how you will and will not provide support during exposure tasks. In some instances, your role may involve being an active cheerleader, providing verbal and emotional support and encouragement as your loved one engages in the perceived risks of exposure and ritual prevention. At other times, you could serve as more of a silent support. This role might require that you remain close during the exposure task, but passively wait for your loved one to ask for your assistance if needed. In other, more difficult exposure tasks, your part may require you to serve as a supportive role model by engaging in the exposure along with your loved one. In yet other instances, you will focus on the difficult task of resisting urges to provide reassurance or accommodating behaviors as you have done in the past.

OCD Feeding Chart

Proposed solutions	Feeds OCD	Does Not Feed OCD
1. _____	_____	_____
2. _____	_____	_____
3. _____	_____	_____
4. _____	_____	_____
5. _____	_____	_____
6. _____	_____	_____
7. _____	_____	_____
8. _____	_____	_____

Remember that the preplanned strategy of contracting is intended to create opportunities for responding to OCD moments instead of just reacting to them. Responding to OCD moments allows everyone to feel more in control while working together to fight the OCD. Reacting to OCD results in everyone feeling badly, while interfering with the goal of freedom from the grips of OCD. You have seen the negative reactions often associated with OCD moments. You can thus see the need to turn down the volume on emotional reactivity and negativity. In this way, you can be more effective in your loved one's recovery.

If your loved one isn't actively fighting back against the OCD, you can still use contracting to help free yourself from the grips of OCD. In chapter 10, you'll learn how to build family resilience. This will help you cope with the stress of dealing with OCD. Chapter 11 will aid you as you encourage your loved one to seek further help. Read these chapters and set goals that will help you in your struggle with OCD.

REWARD YOURSELF

An important part of the contracting process is identifying rewards for successful completion of contract goals. Specify what you will earn for meeting goal behaviors, how much, and at what point in time it will be awarded. Encourage your loved one to develop a reward wish list that includes material and nonmaterial rewards for meeting his or her ERP goals. In the same way, develop your own reward wish list. Each family member needs to be rewarded for meeting goals. Alternatively, rewards can be activities or items shared by the entire family. Rewards should serve to motivate each family member in the fight against OCD, as well as recognize the courage and strength required to accomplish the contracted goal. Examples of rewards are dinner out at a special restaurant, tickets to a game or show, a new outfit, a long-desired golf club, or a weekend vacation.

MODIFYING CONTRACTS

It's essential to approach contracting in a fluid and flexible manner. The contract should continually change as everyone makes progress in your efforts against OCD. You may need to break some short-term goals further down into even smaller goals if efforts at upholding the contract aren't successful. You will make changes to the contract as you monitor how the new responses work over time. When you complete a new behavior for an agreed-upon amount of time, you have achieved your goal. If your loved one accepts this alternative response, move on to the next goal on the target date. In this way, you will move through the short-term goals of your contract.

With contracting, your loved one is encouraged and supported by the family but is also given the responsibility of confronting the fears and resisting rituals or other avoidance behaviors. Together you cocreate a road map for change founded upon communication and respect for the anxiety involved with OCD. Contracting is an effective strategy that not only reduces tension between family members but also serves as a powerful and collaborative force in gaining independence from OCD.

Here is a blank contract for you to use, followed by an example contract filled out by two brothers. Be sure to carefully review the example before attempting to do a contract with your loved one. Make copies of the blank contract so you can write a new contract when you've accomplished your first long-term goal. The next two chapters also include examples of contracts for you to study as models.

Family Contract

Today's date: _____   Target date: _____

Problem: _____

_____

_____

Long-term goal: _____

_____

Reward: _____

_____

Short-term goal 1. _____

_____

Anxiety level: _____   When/frequency: _____

Target date: _____   Date completed: _____

Refrain from: _____

_____

Respond alternatively with: _____

_____

_____

_____

Reward: _____

_____

Short-term goal 2. _____

_____

Anxiety level: _____   When/frequency: _____

Target date: _____   Date completed: _____

Refrain from: _____

_____

Respond alternatively with: _____

_____

_____

_____

_____

Reward: _____

_____

Short-term goal 3. _____

_____

Anxiety level: _____   When/frequency: _____

Target date: _____   Date completed: _____

Refrain from: _____

_____

Respond alternatively with: _____

_____

_____

_____

_____

Reward: _____

_____

Short-term goal 4. _____

_____

Anxiety level: _____   When/frequency: _____

Target date: _____   Date completed: _____

Refrain from: _____

_____

Respond alternatively with: _____

_____

_____

_____

_____

Reward: _____

_____

Short-term goal 5. _____

_____

Anxiety level: _____   When/frequency: _____

Target date: _____   Date completed: _____

Refrain from: _____

_____

Respond alternatively with: _____

_____

_____

_____

_____

Reward: _____

_____

Short-term goal 6. _____

_____

Anxiety level: _____   When/frequency: _____

Target date: _____   Date completed: _____

Refrain from: _____

_____

Respond alternatively with: _____

_____

_____

_____

_____

Reward: _____

_____

Signature: _____

Signature: _____

Signature: _____

JEFF AND MARIO DELANEY'S FAMILY CONTRACT

Mario had cleaning rituals related to contamination fears, both at work and at home. Mario's siblings and parents had been involved with his OCD, and the family was trying to find a way out of this OCD distress. They were trying to find ways to support him more effectively. Mario had struggled with his OCD for many years. When he turned thirty-five, he decided he'd had enough of this way of life. With the support of his family, he committed to cognitive behavioral therapy with a therapist.

Mario and his family also developed some family contracts. First, Mario's family members assessed their roles in accommodating the OCD, using the exercises that were given earlier in this chapter. Then they found a non-OCD moment to discuss the information they had gathered.

Mario's brother Jeff was very involved in accommodating Mario's OCD fears at the family store, so Jeff and Mario decided to work closely on limiting the accommodating behavior. The accommodating log was an objective view for them to see Jeff's protective nature in action.

The brothers identified a problem area to work on together and then identified a long-term goal. After brainstorming options, they thought about the consequences for possibly feeding OCD or not. Finally, they broke down the contract into several steps, or short-term goals, and agreed on a plausible time line with target dates for achieving them. Mario wrote down his level of anxiety for each short-term goal, and they hammered out the rest of the contract based on all of the gathered information. Jeff's long-term goal was to stop participating in rituals and reassurance at the office. Jeff wanted to remove himself from the accommodating role of feeding OCD.

Mario welcomed his brother's help at work and his parents' help at home. Jeff had always tried to help him stay calm at work. Now he was working on facing his fears and was ready for Jeff's help. Mario knew that Jeff could help him with his therapy by encouraging him to constantly expose himself to his fears. Jeff would then be helping Mario rather than the OCD.

Jeff was encouraged by Mario's progress in therapy and gratified to discover he could help his brother fight back against the OCD. He regretted his contribution to his brother's OCD, but now that they were both armed with knowledge, he felt they could face the challenges ahead and respond differently to the demands of OCD. He knew that they could show the OCD a thing or two. Mario could prove that he didn't need to listen to the OCD messages and feel scared. He'd been working on his contamination fears with exposure work, and now Jeff could help him by providing further exposures. Jeff was relieved to have a better way to be supportive of Mario.

The contract they worked on targeted the contamination fears. They agreed on an alternative verbal response of uncertainty that would not reassure and feed the OCD. They also agreed on behavioral ways to expose Mario to his fears in ways that he was ready to address.

Mario's family members were all feeling more aware of how they had been trying to help him stay calm. Their parents supported Jeff and Mario as they worked through the contracting process at work. Mario and his parents used the contracting process to tackle accommodation problems they were experiencing at home. Chapter 8 includes Mario's contract with his parents. Here is the contract that Jeff and Mario devised together.

Jeff and Mario's Family Contract

Today's date: _January 1_   Target date: _January 24_

Problem: _Jeff's helping to feed OCD by participating in cleaning rituals, reassurance,_ _and avoidance of OC triggers._

Long-term goal: _Eliminate participation in cleaning rituals, reassurance. Provide_ _exposures for Mario to promote his recovery. Remove Mario from role of_ _accommodating/feeding the OCD at the office._

Reward: _Tickets to basketball game_

Short-term goal 1. _Jeff will wipe hands with wet cloth before entering office,_ _reassure one time, then give alternative response._

Anxiety level: _45_   When/frequency: _Each work day_

Target date: _January 1-4_   Date completed: _____

Refrain from: _reassuring repeatedly_

Respond alternatively with: _"I can no longer help you feed the OCD. You're_ _learning not to feed the OCD, so let's not allow the OCD to win this time."_

Reward: *Extra hour off at lunch for Mario and Jeff.*

Short-term goal 2.   *Jeff will wipe hands with wet cloth before entering room, provide no reassurance, then give alternative response.*

Anxiety level: ___50___   When/frequency: ___*Each work day*___

Target date: ___*January 5-7*___   Date completed: _____

Refrain from: ___*reassurance*___

Respond alternatively with: ___*"I can no longer help you feed the OCD. You're learning not to feed the OCD, so let's not allow the OCD to win this time."*___

Reward: ___*Extra hour off at lunch for Mario and Jeff*___

Short-term goal 3.   *Jeff will walk in carrying unused wet cloth, provide no reassurance, then give alternative response.*

Anxiety level: ___60___   When/frequency: ___*Each work day*___

Target date: ___*January 8-10*___   Date completed: _____

Refrain from: ___*cleaning ritual, reassurance*___

Respond alternatively with: ___*"I can no longer help you feed the OCD. You're learning not to feed the OCD, so let's not allow the OCD to win this time. You've been working on contaminating your office, so I may be bringing you more contaminants."*___

Reward: ___*Extra hour off at lunch for Mario and Jeff*___

Short-term goal 4.   *One time per hour, Jeff will walk in carrying unused wet cloth, provide no reassurance, then give alternative response.*

Anxiety level: ___65___   When/frequency: ___*Each work day*___

Target date: ___*January 11-14*___   Date completed: _____

Refrain from: ___*cleaning ritual, reassurance*___

Respond alternatively with: ___*"I can no longer help you feed the OCD. You are learning not to feed the OCD, so let's not allow the OCD to win this time. You've been working on contaminating your office, so I may be bringing you more contaminants."*___

Reward: ___*Extra hour off at lunch for Mario and Jeff*___

Short-term goal 5.   *Two times per hour, Jeff will walk in carrying unused wet cloth, provide no reassurance, then give alternative response.*

Anxiety level: ___70___   When/frequency: ___Each work day___

Target date: ___January 15-19___   Date completed: _____

Refrain from: ___cleaning ritual, reassurance___

Respond alternatively with: ___"I can no longer help you feed the OCD. You are___ ___learning not to feed the OCD, so let's not allow the OCD to win this time. You've___ ___been working on contaminating your office, so I may be bringing you more contaminants."___

Reward: ___Extra hour off at lunch for Mario and Jeff___

Short-term goal 6. ___Two times per hour, Jeff will walk in carrying unused wet cloth___ ___and carrying an item from the store, provide no reassurance, then give alternative response.___

Anxiety level: ___75___   When/frequency: ___Each work day___

Target date: ___January 20-24___   Date completed: _____

Refrain from: ___cleaning ritual, reassurance___

Respond alternatively with: ___"I can no longer help you feed the OCD. You are___ ___learning not to feed the OCD, so let's not allow the OCD to win this time. You've___ ___been working on contaminating your office, so I may be bringing you more contaminants."___

Reward: ___Extra hour off at lunch for Mario and Jeff___

Signature: ___Jeff___

Signature: ___Mario___

Summary

Behavioral contracts can help you respond differently to OCD and progress toward freedom from its grip. After reading this chapter, negotiate a contract between you and your loved one, using the following guidelines:

- Identify the day-to-day areas or situations that are made more difficult because of your loved one's OCD by completing the Impact of OCD chart.

- List the reoccurring activities and situations that are made more difficult because of your loved one's OCD on the Difficult Situations chart.

- Record the number of times per day that you engage in accommodating behavior on the Frequency of Accommodating Behaviors chart.

- List the different OCD situations in which you react with an accommodating behavior on the Accommodating Behavior Log.

- Use the Feelings Diary to become more aware of the emotional impact of OCD.

- After completing the charts, agree with your loved one about a problem area for contracting, and then identify and define the long-term goal related to that problem.

- Together with your loved one, identify smaller steps that can be made in the direction of your long-term goal. Arrange these short-term goals in order of increasingly difficult exposures.

- Use the OCD Feeding Chart to help you evaluate your options for responding differently and avoiding feeding the OCD.

- Identify rewards for successful completion of contract goals.

- Make copies of the blank Family Contract. Complete and sign a contract between you and your loved one.

- Make changes to the contract as you monitor how the new responses work over time.

Chapter 8

Parents, Siblings, and Friends: Partners in Recovery

As a parent, sister, brother, or friend, you have a unique relationship with your loved one who has OCD. You have seen and experienced the many negative effects of OCD on relationships. Your responses to OCD can have both negative and positive effects on recovery. Again, contracting can help both you and your loved one become more independent and less ruled by the demands of OCD. Your relationship will be strengthened by achieving mutual goals and fighting the OCD, rather than feeding the OCD. You can then move forward, nourish your relationship, and base it on interests and goals other than OCD.

This chapter continues to show you how contracting works. First, it will take a look at the contract that Mario and his parents developed for responding differently to OCD at home. Then it will discuss trouble spots that you may face as you react or respond to OCD situations.

MARIO DELANEY'S CONTRACT WITH HIS PARENTS

At age thirty-five, Mario still lived with his parents, Louis and Rose. As you may recall, Mario's cleaning and washing rituals included reassurance seeking and various accommodations by family members, both at work and at home. His family was trying to find a way out of their distress and participation in the OCD cycle while supporting Mario in his cognitive behavioral therapy.

Mario had struggled with OCD since childhood. He didn't want to waste another year living under the rules of OCD. As Mario began therapy for OCD, his family members learned about how their accommodating behaviors had been affecting the OCD. Both Mario and his parents were ready to approach OCD in an entirely new way. He was ready to include them in his new risk-taking approach (ERP) to OCD. Mario's parents were ready to view their well-intentioned accommodations as part of the OCD cycle.

Again, the first step in the contracting process is to identify the problem area: what are some of the day-to-day situations that are made more difficult due to OCD? Using the self-monitoring logs and charts that were introduced in chapter 7, Mario's parents began assessing the problem areas, their roles in accommodating, and the related emotions. They had always had a close relationship with Mario, and they had always been very protective of him. The Accommodating Behavior Log provided an objective view of their protective nature in action.

After completing the self-monitoring exercises, Mario and his parents sat down together and discussed what they had learned about their role in accommodating Mario's OCD. They were now able to identify recurring problematic situations and areas for change. They discussed challenging situations and agreed on the first problem area to address. Their first contract targeted the parents' accommodations of Mario's avoidance and the time-consuming washing rituals that immediately followed his return home from work each day.

Louis had accommodated Mario's OCD by opening the front door to the house as they returned home from work together. This allowed Mario to avoid spreading the contamination from work around the house, which he considered "safe." After entering the house, Rose would greet Mario at the kitchen sink with a bottle of liquid anti-bacterial soap. She accommodated Mario's OCD by dispensing the soap into Mario's hands and then turning the faucets on and off as needed. These accommodations allowed Mario to wash away the day's contamination and to avoid becoming recontaminated as a result of touching the kitchen faucets. Over the years, they had developed these routines to save time and help control Mario's anxiety.

Since Mario's parents' accommodations were so intertwined, they decided to combine their efforts and develop one contract with Mario. Their long-term goal was to eliminate their participation in Mario's avoidance and washing rituals upon his return home from work and to encourage Mario to take risks by engaging in exposures. Mario's parents broke down their long-term goal into several smaller steps, or short-term goals. They made sure that with each progressive short-term goal, they were feeding the OCD less and less. Mario then assigned an anxiety level to each of the short-term goals on the contract and they agreed on a plausible time line for achieving the goals, filling in target dates on the contract.

The last step was to identify rewards or incentives for successful completion of their long-term and short-term goals. Remember that it's important to recognize your and your loved one's efforts in making these difficult changes and paving the way for a life free from OCD. Mario and his parents decided on dinner at a nice restaurant for meeting their long-term goal. For meeting short-term goals, they rewarded themselves by taking turns cooking special meals for each other. This added a little fun and even helped them develop a shared interest outside of OCD. Louis, Rose, and Mario improved their eating habits and took pride in their abilities to prepare and serve great meals.

Louis, Rose, and Mario's Family Contract

Today's date: *January 1*   Target date: *January 24*

Problem: *Louis and Rose have been helping to feed Mario's OCD each day as he returns home from work by accommodating his avoidance and washing rituals.*

Long-term goal: *Louis and Rose will eliminate their participation in Mario's avoidance and washing rituals upon his return home from work. They will also provide support and encouragement for Mario to engage in risk taking and exposures.*

Reward: *Dinner at a nice restaurant*

Short-term goal 1. *Mario will open the door to the house himself when he arrives home from work, thus contaminating the door handle with contamination from work. Rose will temporarily continue to assist Mario with the soap dispenser and faucets.*

Anxiety level: *35*   When/frequency: *Each work day*

Target date: *January 1-4*   Date completed: _____

Refrain from: *Louis will refrain from opening the house door for Mario when they arrive home from work. Louis and Rose will refrain from providing reassurance if Mario asks for it.*

Respond alternatively with: *"I know this is difficult for you, but you can take the risk. You can learn to live with the idea that you are contaminating the door handle with germs from work. You could get sick as a result of spreading it, but getting sick for a couple of days is better than living the OCD way for the rest of your life."*

Reward: *Rose prepares a special meal.*

Short-term goal 2: *In addition to continuing the previous exposure, Louis, Rose, and Mario will purposely spread work contamination around the living room at home. Rose will temporarily continue to assist Mario with the soap dispenser and faucets.*

Anxiety level: *55*   When/frequency: *Each work day*

Target date: *January 5-7*   Date completed: _____

Refrain from: *Louis and Rose will refrain from reassuring Mario that it is okay to spread the contamination in the living room.*

Respond alternatively with: *"I know this is difficult for you, but you can take the risk. You can learn to live with the idea that you are contaminating the house with germs from work. You could get sick as a result, but getting sick for a couple of days is better than living the OCD way for the rest of your life."*

Reward: *Louis prepares a special meal*

Short-term goal 3: *In addition to previous exposures, Mario will touch and use the soap dispenser and faucets himself.*

Anxiety level: *65*   When/frequency: *Each work day*

Target date: *January 8-10*   Date completed: _____

Refrain from: *Louis and Rose will continue to refrain from reassuring Mario that it is okay to spread the contamination in the living room, and Rose will refrain from assisting Mario with the soap dispenser and faucets.*

Respond alternatively with: *"I know this is difficult for you, but you can take the risk. You can learn to live with the idea that you are contaminating the house with germs from work. You could get sick as a result of spreading it, but getting sick for a couple of days is better than living the OCD way for the rest of your life."*

Reward: *Mario prepares a special meal.*

Short-term goal 4: *In addition to previous exposures, Louis, Rose, and Mario will purposely spread work contamination around the entire home, except Mario's bedroom, creating more opportunities for Mario to expose himself to work contamination at home.*

Anxiety level: *70*   When/frequency: *Each work day*

Target date: *January 11-14*   Date completed: _____

Refrain from: *Louis and Rose will continue to refrain from reassuring Mario that it is okay to spread the contamination around the home.*

Respond alternatively with: *"I know this is difficult for you, but you can take the risk. You can learn to live with the idea that you are contaminating the house with germs from work. You might get sick as a result of spreading it, but getting sick for a couple of days is better than living the OCD way for the rest of your life."*

Reward: *Rose prepares a special meal.*

Short-term goal 5: *In addition to the previous exposures, Mario will refrain from washing when he returns home from work.*

Anxiety level: *75* When/frequency: *Each work day*

Target date: *January 15-19* Date completed: _____

Refrain from: *Louis and Rose will continue to refrain from reassuring Mario that it is okay to spread the contamination around the home.*

Respond alternatively with: *"I know this is difficult for you, but you can take the risk. You can learn to live with the idea that you are contaminating the house with germs from work. You could get sick as a result of spreading it, but getting sick for a couple of days is better than living the OCD way for the rest of your life."*

Reward: *Louis prepares a special meal.*

Short-term goal 6: *In addition to the previous exposures, Louis, Rose, and Mario will purposely spread work contamination around the entire home, including Mario's bedroom.*

Anxiety level: *80* When/frequency: *Each work day*

Target date: *January 20-24* Date completed: _____

Refrain from: *Louis and Rose will continue to refrain from reassuring Mario that it is okay to spread the contamination around the home.*

Respond alternatively with: *"I know this is difficult for you, but you can take the risk. You can learn to live with the idea that you are contaminating the house with germs from work. You could get sick as a result of spreading it, but getting sick for a couple of days is better than living the OCD way for the rest of your life."*

Reward: *Mario prepares a special meal.*

Signature: *Mario*

Signature: *Louis*

Signature: *Rose*

Mario recognized how his parents had always tried to help make his evenings easier by helping him out with his rituals after work. But now that he was working on facing his fears, he was also ready to take risks with their support. He knew that their encouraging him to constantly expose himself to his contamination fears was the best way for his parents to be helpful. They would be assisting Mario rather than assisting the OCD. Louis and Rose saw how dedicated Mario was to working on his contamination fears with exposure work and were thankful for the opportunity to help him by also providing exposures. They were relieved to have a better way to be supportive of him.

PARTNERS IN RECOVERY

Whether you are a parent, sister, brother, or friend, it's important that you and your loved one think of yourselves as partners in the battle against OCD. Parents of adults play a far different role from parents of children. Their role is an important one, but it is more of a partnering role than a parenting role in the recovery process. Again, when it comes to the fight against OCD, it's best for family members to view themselves as partners. Much of the advice in this chapter also applies when a parent has OCD. Cherry's son James was greatly instrumental in her recovery, for example.

Important family issues tend to arise in many families affected by OCD. Loved ones report the uncertainty that they feel when they make choices about how they react to the OCD. They may get caught between an intuitive desire to protect the person with OCD and a vague feeling that they might be feeding the anxiety. Families often feel trapped in the ways that they react to the OCD. Some family attributes (and their associated reactions to OCD) tend to interfere with the recovery from OCD. Certain family attributes also make it more challenging to maintain recovery gains. The rest of this chapter will discuss trouble spots that can occur in different areas. In the pages ahead, you'll be asked to examine your situation for difficulties in each of these areas.

Modeling Reactions

Children model their behavior on their parents' styles of coping or reacting to stress. For example, a mother may hold her head in her hands and cry, or she may respond calmly and discuss various ways to solve a problem. Depending on whether the mother reacts in the former or latter manner, her children will learn different things. As adults, people continue to model their behavior on other people's reactions, including their parents' reactions.

It can be beneficial for people with OCD to imitate the behavior of those they trust. As a parent with OCD, Cherry found that she could benefit from observing her son's behavior, as well as her husband's. Her son James was twelve years old when she developed OCD, but he was old enough to be very supportive. She trusted him and felt safe modeling her reactions on his. Cherry had fears that she would contaminate other people's food. She lost track of what was "normal" behavior. Touching chips or unwrapped candy that someone else might later eat was a big challenge for her. What if she contaminated them and others became sick? She copied her son's behavior as he put his hand in the bowl of potato chips at a party. He helped her feel okay with touching unwrapped candies or chips.

Modeling your adaptive coping responses can be helpful to your loved one. However, modeling anxiety-ridden or negative reactions is not helpful. The contracting process is an important way for family members and friends to model their adaptive coping skills. Your loved one can learn from your skills. As you go through the contracting process and increase your understanding of accommodating behavior, you send the message that you feel confident about your loved one's ability to cope more effectively. Prior to this, in your day-to-day life, you may have been inadvertently sending the opposite message. Doubting your loved one's competence or ability to handle problems is an anxiety-enhancing behavior. When we doubt or question others' abilities to manage their feelings, we send the message that they can't be trusted to care for themselves.

Developing contracts reduces anxiety because you send the message that you believe in your loved one. Your confidence helps your loved one perform exposures to feared or distressing situations. By communicating confidence in the other person, you enhance the possibility of a successful outcome and help him or her maintain recovery gains over time. Unlike accommodating, this is a strategic way of offering support and is less likely to help maintain or to exacerbate OCD symptoms.

How can you use the concept of modeling as you help your loved one fight OCD?

_____

_____

_____

_____

How do you doubt your loved one's competence?

_____

_____

_____

_____

How do you encourage confidence in his or her ability to cope more effectively?

_____

_____

_____

_____

When Others Are Anxious or Depressed

Sometimes family members and friends have difficulty understanding how they are contributing to OCD. Family members may unwittingly limit exposures by their own anxiety-enhancing behaviors. Also, those who themselves have OCD or another psychiatric disorder can interfere with progress toward recovery. A family member's own difficulty with anxiety or depression may influence the loved one's perception and anticipation of danger. For instance, an older parent's excessive warnings or worries may cause even an adult child to overestimate the possibility of danger.

When people are themselves suffering from depression or anxiety, they react to problems differently from how they might react with less distress. Anxious or depressed people can respond in a more threatened fashion because they interpret situations as more threatening. They see the "what-ifs?" or possible threats of ambiguous situations and make decisions accordingly. They often respond in their own avoidant manner as well, keeping clear of situations that they perceive as threatening or anxiety provoking. Avoidance, as a solution to a problem, can make for poor family problem-solving and decision-making. If your loved one observes you avoiding situations, he or she may feel similar stress and use avoidance as a possible solution. Again, for the person with OCD, a typical response to stress is often either avoidance or ritualizing.

A family member's anxiety may interfere with exposure homework. For instance, homework may include touching toilet seats, and family members may not encourage the person with OCD to touch the seat because of their own fear of catching a disease. Alternatively, they may help the person find strategies for the exposure to get watered down, such as using a glove, cleaning the seat first, or encouraging the touching of the seemingly least used toilet in the public bathroom. They may not implement the exposure homework to the letter, or exactly right, making changes along the way that support OCD fears and symptoms.

Anxious or depressed family members or friends also may not be as responsive to the needs of the person with OCD. They may have limited tolerance for their own anxiety during exposure assignments or may not be able to provide the support and encouragement that the person with OCD needs during the treatment process and beyond. The person with OCD feels the lack of support and may as a result have trouble implementing the exposure work.

An anxious family member may avoid objects or situations as well. What if the person with OCD needs to go to a mall for exposure work, and the family member has anxiety in crowded places? It might become easier to just avoid this exposure work, or the distress may become too high for either person to handle. The person with OCD sees the family member avoiding and learns that this is a necessary or acceptable response to anxiety.

Often, when one family member seeks help for OCD or another psychiatric disorder, other family members see their own problems with anxiety or depression more clearly. This can be the needed incentive for seeking help for themselves. Explore the effects of anxiety and depression in your family on the Effects of Anxiety and Depression of Others on OCD chart.

Effects of Anxiety and Depression of Others on OCD

If you experience anxiety or depression, how might it be affecting your family member's OCD?

_____

_____

_____

_____

If you experience anxiety or depression, how might it be affecting your family member's recovery?

_____

_____

_____

If another family member experiences anxiety or depression, how might it be affecting your family member with OCD?

_____

_____

_____

_____

If another family member experiences anxiety or depression, how might it be affecting the recovery of your family member with OCD?

_____

_____

_____

_____

Overprotectiveness

Family members and friends can become quite accustomed to pointing out dangerous or hazardous situations in normal, everyday life. It's a natural tendency to help a loved one avoid anxiety-provoking situations. There's also a desire to avoid family distress. You may lose sight of how often you are warning your loved one of threats and raising the perception of danger in the environment. Danger becomes generalized, creating general threats or perceptions of threat of unusual things or events. It can also become controlling, in the messages of "Don't do this" and "Watch out for that."

An overprotective atmosphere encourages people with OCD to develop a lower tolerance for uncertainty. Their perception and anticipation of danger is heightened. They may overestimate the probability of danger. Overprotection can become a block toward treatment gains. Conquering OCD is all about taking risks.

Protective behavior can include encouraging less uncomfortable exposure assignments or discouraging distressing exposure assignments. When overprotective and anxious during exposure work, family members can inadvertently make remarks that have a negative impact on the exposure.

Joan sought reassurance from her friends and parents that she hadn't hurt someone by doing something harmful or forgetting to do something she thought she should have done. Every evening she'd go over the day's events and invariably come up with a scenario by which she could have caused harm or put someone in danger. Perhaps she'd said something that hurt a friend's feelings. This warranted a phone call to check on her friend. One evening she became worried when she suddenly realized that she hadn't listened for the toilet to stop flushing when she left the bathroom at work. She usually stopped before leaving the bathroom and listened to make sure the toilet was okay. What if it overflowed?

Joan's father had also struggled with OCD. He'd received cognitive behavioral therapy and liked to say he was "95 percent cured." Some of his daughter's scenarios made sense to him. He found himself getting wrapped up in her rituals, offering reassurance even though he knew that wasn't the best thing for her. He was reluctant to support her when she decided to resist ruminating over the day's events. It made sense to him to go over things at least once, and he didn't mind "helping." Finally, he agreed that it was important for Joan to stop going over the day's events and that it was also important for him to resist offering reassurance when she did seek it from him. Together, they developed a response he could give when she asked for reassurance that she hadn't caused harm: "I can't comment on that. You may or may not have caused harm, but we'll both have to live with the uncertainty. Resisting this ritual will help both of us fight our OCD." It was important for Joan and her father to recognize that reassurance seeking was a ritual, and for him, giving the reassurance and joining her in her checking rituals were also rituals.

Before joining her with her fight with the OCD, Joan's father would say such things as, "Maybe you should call and make sure Tina's not angry. It wouldn't hurt." Or, "Call the store and have someone check the toilet." Such remarks place the seed of doubt that helps the OCD to grow. Her father's comments made Joan think that there really were dangers. This strengthened the OCD and weakened Joan's resolve. Instead of protecting your family member during exposure work, it's better to encourage risk taking.

When feeling anxious, it's harder to remember that the goal is long-term change. In a typical exposure session, the short-term anxiety can be overwhelming to family members. They may forget about the long-term gratification and become focused on short-term relief. In this way, they may curtail or decrease the exposure homework assignments because of their own anxiety and need to protect their loved ones from distress or discomfort. Remember, the therapeutic goal is to live through the short-term distress for long-term relief.

List some of your experiences when you may have been overprotective of your loved one.

_____

_____   _____

_____

_____

Differences in Each Family Member's Perspective on OCD

It's common for familial conflict to increase in homes where OCD lives. Conflict may arise from family members' different perspectives on how to handle OCD difficulties. One person may tend to be more enmeshed, and another may be more hostile and distant, each choosing different ways of handling stressful situations. With adult children, sometimes one parent has an interest in keeping the grown child at home and gets continued rewards from parenting. The parent's behavior reinforces the message that the adult child is incapable of independence. Both parent and child may fear and feel threatened by the possibility of living independently (or alone and uncared for). Likewise, siblings and even close friends can find fulfillment in caring for a person with OCD and maintaining the dependency.

The contracting process helps improve communication about important issues, family roles, and needs. Examining accommodating behaviors helps you see the similarities and differences in your beliefs and expectations, as well as in your perspectives on how to handle the problems.

How might family members' perspectives on OCD be different in your family?

_____

_____

_____

_____

Working as a Team

Working as a team is one of the central ways that families can help. Whether it's teamwork engaging in exposures, minimizing avoidance tactics, decreasing accommodating behaviors, or implementing the reward system, the team approach works best for recovery. Rewards can be a source of conflict, however. Sometimes implementing the reward system can become a struggle for the family, thus creating extra conflict and tension. It's important to clarify rewards as a family before implementing the contract. You may want to seek help from a more objective third party to decrease the conflict at home, minimize interference with the contract, and focus on the OCD. This could be a therapist or a trusted friend. Over time, the third party can transfer responsibility to family members as the contracting process becomes more stable and understood by the family.

What concerns do you have about using a reward system with your family member?

_____

_____

_____

_____

Excessive Self-Sacrifice

A central theme running through many accommodating behaviors is self-sacrifice. The issue of self-sacrifice is an important issue for parents with an adult child living at home. You may expect to sacrifice for your teen, but there are a myriad of feelings and worries when sacrifice continues into your child's twenties and thirties. Keep in mind that families are dealing with this even when their adult child does not have OCD. Kids not leaving home is a growing issue. Self-sacrifice can also be a problem for siblings, close friends, and adult children of a parent who has OCD.

There are many feelings involved in such imbalanced relationships. When people sacrifice to an excessive degree for someone else, resentment, worry, and frustration can be the result. Family members may inappropriately lean toward martyrdom, leading to resentment and hostility toward the loved one over time. For instance, they may think or say with a hint of exasperation or hostility, "It's all about my child, everything is for my child. I have no time for me."

Some people give up jobs in order to help a loved one with OCD maintain work or school routines and live life beyond the interference of rituals. Perhaps OCD has demanded that you be present and observe rituals—or even participate in the rituals—to decrease your loved one's distress. You give in to the demands of OCD, sacrificing time and energy you need to fulfill other responsibilities and care for other members of your family.

Cherry's son was sympathetic and tried not to show his distress when he was late for school because of his mother's checking and rechecking the appliances and door. As she practiced ERP and he learned more about OCD, he realized his sacrificing was actually detrimental to his mother's recovery. He told Cherry that being late for school was upsetting and embarrassing. Recognizing how her behavior affected her son encouraged Cherry to implement ERP and take risks.

In what ways do you believe you sacrifice excessively for your family member?

_____

_____

_____

_____

Describe the positive and negative effects of being self-sacrificing.

_____

_____

_____

_____

Overinvolvement

Sometimes family members make intrusive comments, assuming they understand the feelings of the person with OCD. They may tell the person how he or she must be feeling, with little interest in or desire to listen to how the person actually feels. Instead of asking, "How are you feeling?" a family member might declare, "I know you're really scared and embarrassed. You can't deny it." Such comments are inappropriately intrusive and don't allow for the autonomy of the other person. An excessive degree of emotional involvement can feel overbearing and suffocating.

Emotional overinvolvement can also take the form of excessive emotional concern for the loved one, apparent in such comments as, "Are you sure you're ready to do that exposure?" instead of "You know best what you're ready for. I'm behind you." This trait can be hard for family members to see in themselves. They care very much about their loved one and want to do all they can to help. Unfortunately, this can become controlling as they suggest to the loved one how he or she feels or should feel, or give unwarranted advice about what should be done. They become overly controlling in a mistaken attempt to save the person from the OCD. Or they might become overly involved with the OCD symptoms, participating in rituals, for example. Without an accurate understanding of OCD, this method backfires. OCD grows as they accommodate the demands through emotional overinvolvement and self-sacrifice.

In what ways do you become emotionally overinvolved in your loved one's OCD?

_____

_____

_____

_____

Expressing Criticism

Family members sometimes resort to criticism in a misguided attempt to help their loved one. They think that if they tell the person how to do things differently, that they will solve the problems. While your loved one is struggling with OCD, they hear these messages and perceive the criticism in your remarks. It stings rather than feels loving, productive, and helpful. Criticism can have a detrimental effect on your loved one and can have a negative effect on treatment. After hearing criticism, people can have such negative thoughts as, "Why bother trying to change? I won't be able to do it," or "Nothing will change anyway. No one thinks I can be different," or "Maybe without my OCD getting in the way, I still won't be able to accomplish anything or make them proud of me."

Exposure work is very difficult for people with OCD because they are facing fears; criticism can take the air out of your loved one's sails as he or she works up the courage to take risks. Criticism can be very subtle, such as, "You did part of the exposure homework but not all of it, giving up as usual." You should also avoid nonverbal messages of disappointment (heavy sighs and head shaking) if your loved one does not meet your expectations.

Family members may perceive the person with OCD as lazy, unproductive, selfish, or spoiled, especially if he or she is experiencing difficulty getting motivated to overcome OCD. It can be helpful to become aware of your direct and indirect expressions of these negative judgments. You are learning more about OCD and its overwhelming and overpowering grip on those struggling with it.

Parents and other family members may believe that they can help the person with OCD get better if they just say the right thing to motivate them. This may translate into nagging, excessive prodding, criticism, and hostile remarks. Aggressive, intrusive comments may further create more fear, shame, and anger in your loved one. This can make it less likely that he or she will seek or continue getting treatment. By continuing to learn new ways to respond to and deal with OCD, you can stay involved without becoming overinvolved and critical.

Your loved one needs active support, and hostile criticism is just the opposite. People with OCD need to be boosted up with words of encouragement during the difficult exposure work: "You can do it," "You almost did it," "You did it, wow!" This means cheering them on at tasks that may seem small to you but are challenging and scary for them: touching a doorknob and refraining from washing their hands; messing up the house and refraining from immediately cleaning it up; or throwing out collected things or useless pieces of paper. These may not seem like large accomplishments to most people, but people with OCD and their loved ones grow to understand the magnitude of these achievements.

People can lose motivation to change when living with excessive negative criticism. That motivation to change is at the heart of exposure treatment, because changing requires engaging in distressing activities. The person with OCD needs to approach the very things that he or she most wants to avoid. When you share feelings of resentment or dissatisfaction, it can be quite discouraging. When families can separate the symptoms from the person and cheer the person on to overcome the difficulties, their loved one thrives.

A hostile or critical attitude can also have a negative influence on the person's long-term ability to battle the OCD. Some people will do well in treatment and then return to critical family members and experience a relapse of symptoms. If they engage in a ritual, the resulting criticism can make if difficult to go back to exposure. It may reinforce their sense that they are unable to cope more effectively. Instead of seeing symptom flare-ups as a red flag to perform exposures, they see them only as a failure. The influence may be a family member viewing flare-ups as failure and commenting, "I didn't think the good news would last." Review your tendency to criticize on the Criticism Expression chart.

Criticism Expression

How do you express negative thoughts and feelings?

_____

_____

List negative feelings that you experience with regard to your loved one's OCD.

_____

_____

How can you better express these feelings?

_____

_____

List negative thoughts you've had with regard to your loved one's OCD.

_____

_____

_____

_____

How can you better express these thoughts?

_____

_____

By expressing positive feelings and thoughts, you will help your loved one recover from the grips of OCD. Positive feelings can include feelings such as hope, encouragement, concern, and empathy. Positive thoughts and feelings can be expressed in many ways—through praise, words of encouragement, and nonverbal communication (physical affection or eye contact).

The value of expressing positive support should not be overlooked or taken for granted. People absorb both positive and negative feelings, and it's much better when they have more positive ones to soak up. Positive feelings are reinforcing and healing and multiply exponentially when shared. In the same way, negative feelings can make it more difficult to feel good about each other. Review your tendency to express positive feelings and thoughts in the Expressing Positive Support chart.

Expressing Positive Support

List positive feelings about your loved one that you've experienced.

_____

_____

List positive thoughts about your loved one that you've had.

_____

_____

How do you express these positive thoughts and feelings as affirmations?

_____

_____

_____

List opportunities you've had in the last week to offer affirmations to your loved one.

_____

_____

_____

_____

WHAT IF THE PARENT HAS OCD?

For parents with OCD, one of the biggest fears is that their OCD will harm their children. This was a great fear for Cherry. Would the burden of dealing with her OCD cause her son James permanent harm? In some ways, their roles were reversed. James became Cherry's helper when she felt she should be his helper. She turned to him for reassurance when her OCD was at its worst. As Cherry learned more about OCD, she shared information with her husband, as well as her son. James learned not to give reassurance or participate in checking rituals. He watched Cherry apply cognitive behavioral therapy to her symptoms and break free from OCD.

James said, "I'm proud of my mother. Some people would have given up in her situation, but she didn't. She taught me the importance of determination. I've learned from her example and follow it whenever I come across an encounter I feel I can't overcome."

Rather than causing harm, participating in his mother's recovery was a positive influence on James. His accomplishments in this area helped to build his conviction that he could accomplish even more in his life. Watching Cherry recover, then reach out and help others, inspired James and gave him confidence that he too could overcome adversity and help others. Even while coping with his mother's OCD, James did very well in high school, earning several scholarships to college, where he graduated magna cum laude. Then he began a career educating others about the AIDS pandemic in Africa.

OCD does not have to harm a parent's relationship with his or her children. Many families live with some type of conflict or adversity. Adversity can strengthen children and create resilience and coping skills that are useful for more general conflicts and adversity in life. Children and teens can assist their recovering parent in most of the same ways that older family members can. Include them as partners in recovery.

Summary

As a parent, sister, brother, friend, or child of someone with OCD, you are a partner in your loved one's battle against OCD. Together, you can defeat OCD. Review each trouble spot discussed in this chapter and keep the following guidelines in mind as you use contracting to assist your loved one in the recovery process.

- Support is very important. Be ready to listen to the concerns of your loved one and to respond in a new way.

- Let go of the reassurances you are used to giving out.

- Begin to respond less critically and less demandingly to your loved one.

- Let your loved one know that you understand that he or she is not the OCD and that it is a neuropsychological disorder.

- Understand that you and your loved one will both undergo challenging and stressful times.

- Be firm and consistent in the limits that you set up together, allowing a third party to mediate as needed.

- Strive to normalize the family routine, responsibilities, and roles of each family member.

- Move toward expecting a more equal or age-appropriate share of responsibilities from each family member.

- Communicate directly and empathetically with all family members.

- Be clear in your role within the family—as a parent, sibling, son, daughter.

- Be clear in your role as a positive role model.

- Demonstrate your belief in your loved one's ability to overcome OCD.

- Develop realistic and reasonable expectations for your loved one's journey toward recovery.

Chapter 9

You, Your Spouse, and OCD: Three's a Crowd

Some people enter a long-term committed relationship aware of their loved one's OCD. For others, the revelation of OCD does not occur until after the couple has married or otherwise made a commitment to each other. The way OCD symptoms come to light can impact a couple's relationship as well as the couple's response to OCD symptoms and the contracting process. For the purpose of this chapter, the word "spouse" will refer to a significant other in a long-term relationship. The word "marriage" will be used to describe any long-term committed relationship.

WHEN "FOR BETTER OR WORSE" INCLUDES OCD

Spouses who know about their loved one's OCD prior to marriage knowingly commit to supporting their spouse for better or worse through the many yet unknown trials and tribulations of OCD. They don't always, however, fully understand how these trials might actually present themselves. The context of marriage and living with someone day in and day out can provide a whole new window for viewing OCD and the havoc it can wreak.

Regardless of whether your perception of OCD has changed mildly or drastically as a result of marriage, you now have the opportunity to serve as a primary source of support and motivation to your spouse. The rewards of providing support and making healthy changes in yourself and your relationship will unfold over time as you use the contracting process. Answering the questions on the Changing Perceptions chart will help you reflect on how your perception of the OCD has changed.

Changing Perceptions

How has your perception of OCD and its impact on your spouse changed since you married?

_____

_____

_____

How has your perception of OCD's impact on your relationship changed since you married?

_____

_____

_____

Describe your feelings concerning these changes in your perception of OCD.

_____

_____

_____

_____

How have you coped with these changed perceptions?

_____

_____

_____

_____

"SURPRISE . . . I HAVE OCD"

Some spouses feel shocked and confused when the presence of OCD in the relationship is revealed. They may be shocked by the revelation itself or by their own perceived failure to have recognized the spouse's struggles sooner. If they know little or nothing about the illness, they have no basis for understanding their spouse's fears. They may feel confused about how to respond to seemingly bizarre compulsions. Most certainly, they are unaware of the complex ways in which their reactions may be feeding the OCD.

Others may feel deceived or betrayed by a spouse's failure to have revealed the OCD sooner, especially if OCD has been creating previously unexplainable distress in the relationship. They may feel blindsided by the revelation and angered over the impact of OCD on the relationship. Heartfelt statements such as, "This is not what I signed up for when I got married!" may further complicate the situation.

OCD symptoms are sometimes minimal or subclinical prior to getting married but are exacerbated after marriage. People can experience mild and manageable symptoms before marriage that don't interfere with their daily lives. They may have been more able to respond to simple reassurances and to just shrug off their fears and worries. These symptoms can appear as little worries or quirks and be seen as endearing or cute. For some people, the additional stress (albeit good stress) involved in adjusting to the many changes of married life can eventually interfere with managing OCD symptoms effectively. Eventually the level of distress and symptoms increase until they meet the full criteria for a diagnosis of OCD. The longer this continues without recognition and treatment, the greater the distress and impact on the individual and the relationship. In this case, OCD can take *both* spouses by surprise.

Often an early revelation (or heads-up) about the OCD does not affect the decision to get married. When secrets are kept, however, the spouse is often left feeling unprepared for handling the situation. Hardest of all may be trying to understand *why* the other person did not previously reveal this significant part of his or her life. Questions arise, such as, "Why would someone I have devoted my life to not trust our relationship enough to reveal OCD sooner?" Subsequent issues of distrust and anger can further hinder a couple's ability to work together in getting OCD out of their lives and their relationship.

If you were surprised by the revelation of your loved one's OCD, please answer the questions on the Surprised by OCD chart.

Surprised by OCD

How did you learn of your spouse's OCD?

_____

_____

How did you feel when you learned of your spouse's OCD?

_____

_____

How did you react when you learned of your spouse's OCD?

_____

_____

How did finding out the way you did impact the relationship?

_____

_____

_____

_____

How might this impact your ability to help your spouse through the contracting process and ERP?

_____

_____

_____

How might you overcome these obstacles so that you, your spouse, and your relationship can recover from OCD?

_____

_____

_____

Your Spouse's Dilemma: To Tell or Not to Tell?

There are a number of reasons why someone with OCD may feel unable to reveal OCD symptoms. Many people with OCD experience deep shame and embarrassment about their symptoms and behaviors. Sometimes their greatest fears involve being found out by others. Many fear being viewed as less than competent. Others fear they will be viewed as a less equal partner in the relationship if they reveal the extent of their symptoms and emotional pain. Many also fear being judged or rejected by their loved one. They may worry about being left by their significant other "if I reveal the 'real' me." For these reasons, people sometimes go to great lengths to keep their symptoms and suffering hidden from others, including their significant other. Perhaps the greatest fear of all is that their loved one will view them as being just as crazy as they feel. This may be especially true for people who remain undiagnosed and thus confused and scared by the fears they are experiencing and their responses to them.

Others minimize the impact that OCD has on their lives and their relationships. They may develop an incredible ability to compartmentalize. This method of coping allows them to keep OCD and its effects separate from the rest of their life. Unfortunately, this method of coping serves as a double-edged sword for people with OCD. On the one hand, minimizing allows them to deny the negative effects of OCD and thus protects them from experiencing greater anxiety and distress. This allows the OCD to grow. On the other hand, protecting themselves this way allows them to ignore the effects of OCD that need to be acknowledged before recovery can begin. The trade-off is similar to performing a ritual to ward off greater anxiety and distress. In the short run, minimizing allows them to ward off uncomfortable emotions. In the long run, however, minimizing does nothing to address the problem itself. In fact, it's likely to make the OCD worse. The real problems and the underlying cause are left to continue growing and devastating the lives of everyone involved.

Although people may initially not reveal their symptoms out of intense fear or shame, keeping OCD a secret only causes their fear and shame to grow. Thus, the dilemma of "to tell or not to tell" arises. The longer they keep the OCD hidden, the longer they feel they are deceiving their loved one. They feel trapped between the fear of revealing their pain and the fear of keeping it hidden. Such secrets can create a distance that impacts the emotional and physical intimacy of a couple. The burden of this dilemma can interfere with closeness and stifle the growth of the relationship over time. If your spouse kept OCD a secret from you, the Understanding Reluctance to Reveal OCD chart will examine this issue. You may want to discuss the answers with your spouse.

Understanding Reluctance to Reveal OCD

Why do you think your spouse did not reveal the OCD sooner?

_____

_____

_____

_____

Discuss this with your spouse. What reason does he or she give for not revealing the OCD sooner?

_____

_____

_____

_____

Were any of your spouse's concerns or worries about your reactions to this revelation on target?

EFFECTS OF OCD ON A COMMITTED RELATIONSHIP

OCD can have a tremendous impact on your relationship. OCD can interfere with your emotional connection, your physical connection, and the roles in your relationship. OCD can also impact your relationship financially and socially.

Emotional Intimacy

Emotional intimacy refers to a sense of emotional connection that we feel toward another person. This sense of connection allows us to experience trust and safety within relationships. Emotional intimacy allows us to share and disclose aspects of ourselves, our beliefs, and our dreams that we may hide from the rest of the world. It allows us to reach out to our loved ones for help and support in times of need. Emotional intimacy allows us to risk revealing our human vulnerabilities and struggles while trusting that our loved ones will respect and accept our true self.

Emotional intimacy grows over time. Our sense of trust and safety grows each time we share our fears and struggles with our partner, each time we provide or receive support from the other, and each time we celebrate the triumphs of overcoming struggles together.

There are many common everyday challenges and threats to a couple's emotional intimacy. These include external threats, such as stressful situations, limited time together due to time constraints, and daily responsibilities. Internal threats, such as our own personal defenses, mental or physical exhaustion, and unresolved feelings and conflicts, can also interfere with emotional intimacy. Complete the Effects of OCD on Emotional Intimacy chart to get a view of how OCD has affected the emotional intimacy between you and your spouse.

Effects of OCD on Emotional Intimacy

What are some of the external challenges and threats to emotional intimacy in your relationship?

_____

_____

_____

What are some of the internal challenges and threats to emotional intimacy in your relationship?

_____

_____

_____

How might you reduce external challenges and threats to emotional intimacy in your relationship?

_____

_____

_____

How might you reduce internal challenges and threats to emotional intimacy in your relationship?

_____

_____

_____

Threats to emotional intimacy can deplete our reserves of the emotional and physical energy needed to nurture this important aspect of the relationship. For couples affected by OCD, there are even greater threats and challenges to maintaining emotional intimacy. The stresses and responsibilities of daily life don't stand still just because OCD has made its presence known.

You're likely all too aware of how the presence of OCD in your relationship results in a myriad of emotions for each of you. These emotions can be both intense and confusing, and they tend to center around very sensitive areas. When situations such as these exist, spouses may feel compelled to *overfilter*, or hide certain feelings and thoughts from the other. In some instances, this may stem from seemingly good intentions, such as protecting the other person or the relationship from further sources of stress and distress. Overfiltering may also result from self-protection strategies, whereby it helps to minimize emotional risks, vulnerabilities, and threats to self-dignity. Regardless of the spouse's intentions, overfiltering closes off multiple pathways of communication, support, and potential closeness. Thus, the relationship suffers on many levels.

For the spouse who has OCD, feelings of shame or embarrassment may interfere with fully disclosing the extent of fears or the need for additional support. Perceived threats to dignity, independence, or equality within the relationship may result in the spouse holding back and subsequently closing off pathways for obtaining sufficient support. Overfiltering may also occur when the spouse who has OCD attempts to protect the other from further effects of OCD. The spouse with OCD may reason, "My spouse already has so much to deal with because of my OCD. I don't want to make things worse by complaining about how bad my day was." This can make overfiltering an appealing alternative to disclosing the difficult truth.

Similarly, the spouse of the person with OCD may overfilter and hold back, often in an effort to protect the other person from additional sources of stress. The reasoning might be, "I can tell my spouse had a bad day. I'd hate to add to the burden by sharing the stressful events from my workday." Often, people also try to protect the spouse from their own feelings of anger and frustration resulting from OCD situations, reasoning, "Expressing my frustration about OCD will only add to my spouse's stress and make the OCD worse. It's easier to just act like things are okay on my end." Keeping with the notion that "emotional intimacy begets emotional intimacy," it's easy to recognize how this process of overfiltering can hinder a couple's growth together. Complete the Effects of Overfiltering on Emotional Intimacy chart to get a view of how overfiltering has affected the emotional intimacy between you and your spouse.

Effects of Overfiltering on Emotional Intimacy

Your Spouse's Overfiltering

In what ways might your spouse be using overfiltering and why?

_____

_____

In what ways might your spouse's use of overfiltering be affecting emotional intimacy within your relationship?

_____

_____

How might you encourage your spouse to reduce his or her use of overfiltering and thus increase emotional intimacy within your relationship?

_____

_____

Your Overfiltering

In what ways do you use overfiltering and why?

_____

_____

In what ways might your use of overfiltering be affecting emotional intimacy within your relationship?

_____

_____

How could you reduce your use of overfiltering and thus increase emotional intimacy within your relationship?

_____

_____

Physical Intimacy

Physical intimacy is yet another area of relationships that often suffers under the weight of OCD. Obsessive-compulsive disorder can have harmful effects on the couple's physical intimacy in many ways. For those with obsessions and fears about saliva or bodily fluids, the barriers to physical closeness and intimacy are obvious. For those with obsessive fears of harming the spouse, the perceived risk of physical intimacy may overshadow the benefits of physical and emotional closeness. Others are chronically haunted by religious obsessions that are triggered in anticipation of or during moments of physical intimacy. The harmful effects to the couple's relationship are most evident when avoidance of physical intimacy becomes the primary ritual for coping with these and other obsessive fears.

Physical intimacy may become compromised by the daily toll of OCD on each spouse. Living with and coping with OCD on a daily basis can be exhausting. Consider the impact when you factor in the common stressors of everyday life. We have a finite amount of energy available to us each day. When we've depleted our mind and body's energy, the result can be physical, mental, and emotional exhaustion. Any of these forms of exhaustion can result in decreased interest in and desire for physical intimacy.

The cumulative effects of navigating stressful OCD moments can also diminish physical intimacy within the relationship. Hard feelings and resentments resulting from OCD moments can easily threaten each spouse's immediate desire for physical closeness and intimacy. It's not reasonable to expect yourself or your spouse to just turn off these emotions following a difficult OCD situation, nor should that be the goal. It's as important for you each to acknowledge and validate these feelings as it is to resolve them and prevent them from further interfering in the relationship. The contracting process should help to reduce these feelings as you begin working as a team against the OCD. Complete the Effects of OCD on Physical Intimacy chart to get a view of how OCD has affected the physical intimacy between you and your spouse.

Effects of OCD on Physical Intimacy

Which of your spouse's obsessions or compulsions, if any, interfere with physical closeness and intimacy?

_____

_____

_____

How do you cope when obsessions and compulsions interfere with physical closeness and intimacy in the relationship?

_____

_____

_____

How does your spouse cope when obsessions and compulsions interfere with physical closeness and intimacy in the relationship?

_____

_____

_____

Many of the medications prescribed for OCD produce unwanted sexual side effects. Some people report decreased libido, decreased sexual arousal, and diminished ability to reach orgasm. It's important to not personalize or assign blame for any changes in the sexual aspects of your relationship. These issues should be openly discussed between you and your spouse. In some instances, accompanying your spouse to an appointment with the prescribing physician may help you both better understand and navigate these challenges. Review how sexual side effects have affected your relationship on the Effects of Sexual Side Effects chart.

Effects of Sexual Side Effects

What sexual side effects, if any, has your spouse experienced as a result of OCD medication?

_____

_____

_____

How have unwanted sexual side effects impacted physical closeness and intimacy within your relationship?

_____

_____

_____

How thoroughly have you and your spouse discussed with each other the impact of sexual side effects on physical closeness and intimacy within your relationship?

_____

_____

_____

Financial Impact

Money does not buy happiness, but it can alleviate the additional stress and financial strain of pursuing appropriate treatment for OCD. Insurance benefits may help to curb the financial impact of cognitive behavioral therapy sessions with a therapist and medication consultation and management with a psychiatrist, but few insurance companies provide the degree of benefits and resources needed for the optimal treatment of moderate or severe OCD. Invariably, there are out-of-pocket costs involved.

Additional factors can create financial stress. The spouse with OCD may miss hours or even days of work as a result of medical appointments or OCD symptoms. Prescription costs, insurance deductibles, limits to the numbers of sessions allowed in a calendar year, and the duration of adequate OCD treatment can also add to the cost of treatment. Complete the Financial Impact of OCD chart to get a view of how OCD has affected your financial situation.

Financial Impact of OCD

What kinds of limitations or hardships are placed on you and your loved one because of the financial impact of OCD?

_____

_____

_____

How do you cope with any negative feelings or resentments related to the financial impact of OCD?

_____

_____

_____

Scapegoating OCD

When relationships are affected by OCD, it's easy for OCD to become a scapegoat for other sources of marital conflict. The couple may mistakenly attribute all areas of stress and conflict in the relationship to the presence of OCD. This can create unrealistic expectations, perhaps making the couple believe they will find marital bliss once OCD is removed from the equation. This type of thinking gives too much power to the OCD. It also prevents the couple from examining their relationship more closely in order to identify and resolve additional sources of conflict.

It's important for you and your spouse to explore other issues in your relationship that could be causing stress. Take a moment to review the following potential sources of marital conflict and stress and consider how they may be affecting your relationship. Check off the ones that are familiar to you:

- ☐ Differences in communication styles

- ☐ Differences in approaches to problem solving and conflict resolution

- ☐ Aspects of physical intimacy

- ☐ Aspects of emotional intimacy

- ☐ Parenting decisions related to

  - ☐ whether to have children, when? how many?

  - ☐ child discipline

  - ☐ child education

- extending privileges to your children
- Financial decisions such as
    - deciding how to save money
    - deciding how to spend money
    - paying off debts
    - making financial investments
- Decisions related to living arrangements and locations
- Other mental-health issues, such as depression, in either spouse
- Substance abuse by either spouse
- The impact of medical conditions and concerns
- Issues involving extended family members (such as in-laws)
- Occupational decisions
- Extended-family conflicts and demands

It's certainly easy for OCD to function as a distraction or as a scapegoat for other marital stressors. The overall goal for you and your spouse is to deal with the OCD and its impact on the relationship while being mindful of other equally important sources of stress that may be affecting your relationship.

Interference in Marital Roles

In many marriages, OCD can affect the distribution of household responsibilities. Often the spouse who has OCD may develop difficulties fulfilling household responsibilities because these responsibilities trigger obsessions and compulsions. For example, a spouse who has OCD fears of germs and contamination could have great difficulty taking the garbage cans out to the curb, cleaning the bathroom, or washing the laundry. A spouse who has fears of accidentally contaminating or poisoning others might find preparing three meals a day for the family overwhelming. Someone with fears of making a mistake could spend hours balancing the checkbook and writing out checks to pay the bills. Consider, too, the spouse who spends long periods of time checking all the outlets before leaving the home. How might these OCD fears and rituals interfere with leaving the house to run errands, go food shopping, or chauffering the children to their different activities?

Oftentimes, the burden of responsibilities falls on the other spouse. With no end in sight to enduring the stress of these additional responsibilities, the other spouse may become overwhelmed, exhausted, hopeless, and even resentful over time. Meanwhile, the daily reminders of his or her inability to fulfill previously held household responsibilities can leave the spouse who has OCD feeling weak, ashamed, and inadequate—ineffective as a partner in the relationship.

How does OCD interfere with your roles?

_____

_____

_____

_____

Now that you and your spouse are working together to fight against OCD, you can apply the contracting process to regain the former balance in the distribution of responsibilities. Together you can identify problem areas, define short-term goals that support ERP and reduce accommodating behaviors, and eventually work toward longer-term goals that will reestablish balance and decrease stress within your relationship.

Interference in Social Relationships and Activities

OCD can create obstacles to maintaining a social life and participating in activities outside of the marital relationship. Some people with OCD fear becoming stuck in an OCD ritual in public, revealing their dysfunction. They fear others' judgments and the subsequent experience of shame and humiliation. In many instances, they may find it simpler to just avoid such situations and activities. Other social interactions or activities are avoided because they may require contact with an OCD trigger. A person with OCD fears of germs and contamination might find it too difficult to use a public restroom at a restaurant or amusement park. Someone with fears of accidentally harming children might find attending a child's birthday party or baseball game too distressful.

OCD can have a negative impact on both spouses' social relationships and activities. The spouse without OCD may fear the potential for painful and misguided judgments directed toward their loved one. Attending social activities alone due to a loved one's avoidance may not only interfere with your own ability to enjoy the occasion but also may serve as one more painful reminder of OCD's unwelcome presence. The result for the couple is one less experience to share together and the threat of a growing sense of isolation from each other.

You may choose to avoid going to social events alone because you would feel guilty or sad to leave your loved one behind. Offering up creative excuses for declining social invitations and opportunities becomes second nature for some couples. As a result, they may find themselves lonely and withdrawn from people who once held important places in their live—friends and family members alike.

Cherry shared information about her OCD with many of her friends. They offered valuable support as she recovered. Now, they are rejoicing with her about how far she's come in her fight against OCD. Recently, a friend said, "I can tell your OCD is much better. When we first met, you were stiff when someone hugged you. Now, you're more relaxed, and the other day I even saw you initiate a hug with someone." In a culture where everyone hugs, that's an important validation of Cherry's recovery. Cherry didn't realize that her preoccupation with OCD fears had had such an impact on her physical contact with others until her friend mentioned this.

How does OCD interfere with your social relationships and activities?

_____

_____

_____

_____

Would sharing information about your spouse's OCD provide added support? (You should not share information without your spouse's permission.)

_____

_____

_____

_____

Fears for the Future

OCD tends to be a chronic disorder in which symptoms wax and wane over the lifetime. An exacerbation of OCD symptoms can occur in response to a single identifiable stressor or a culmination of life's stressors, while at other times it seemingly comes out of nowhere. The resulting ups and downs of OCD can leave spouses concerned for their future together as a married couple. How will OCD affect our relationship over time? How will we protect our relationship from the challenges of OCD? Are there opportunities that we should not puruse because we fear OCD's potential effects on the future?

One decision that many couples must face is whether or not to have children and assume the responsibilities of parenthood. They may fear the effects of the stress of pregnancy, childbirth, and becoming a parent for the first time. Many also worry about the possibility of their children developing OCD. One or both spouses may fear that OCD will interfere with their ability to be the kind of parent they want to be. They may wonder how the spouse without OCD will cope with added parenting responsibilities should the spouse with OCD experience a relapse of symptoms. Some couples question their capacity to be emotionally and mentally competent parents altogether. In later years, parents may fear what their children are learning and experiencing as they witness countless stressful OCD moments.

What types of OCD-related fears do you have for your future together?

_____

_____

_____

_____

The Stress-Laden Relationship

The cumulative effects of OCD on marriage can result in a relationship burdened by stress and conflict. If left alone, the challenges of OCD moments combined with OCD's threats to the couple's emotional and physical intimacy, related financial stressors, interference in social relationships and activities, and fears for the future can shake the very core of your relationship. Failure to communicate with each other openly about these stressors serves as a form of avoidance that, whether purposeful or inadvertent, creates the opportunity for the roots of the problems to grow while creating even greater opportunity for devastating and painful effects on the relationship.

PARTNERS IN CONTRACTING FOR RECOVERY

Your combined efforts in fighting OCD are a powerful force in reclaiming your lives, your marriage, and your future together. Consider how much stronger you will be as a couple as you learn to communicate and support each other through the challenges of OCD. As you may recall, aspects of emotional intimacy, such as trust and closeness, grow each time we share our fears and struggles, provide or receive support, and celebrate the triumphs of overcoming struggles together. Rather than perceiving OCD's challenges as threats to your marriage, you can begin viewing them as added opportunities for building resiliency and strengthening trust and emotional intimacy. The contracting process will allow you and your spouse to begin making this shift in your thinking about OCD and its effects on your marriage.

SPOUSAL CONTRACTING IN ACTION

Deon's obsessions centered around the fear that he would be responsible for some harm coming to him and his wife by failing to lock the door, or by leaving the computer, lights, stove, or other appliances on. He was late for work quite often because he had to go back to check the door. Deon's wife Alisha accommodated by rearranging her work schedule so that she could leave the house after him, checking everything as she left. When they left the house together, she assisted him in checking, then reassured him that everything was checked well. Often, she reassured him that the door was indeed locked after they left the house. After Deon began treatment and they both learned more about OCD, Alisha realized that there was much she could do to help Deon with his recovery. Together they were determined to run OCD out of their marriage by applying the contracting process.

Identify the Problem Areas

Remember, the first step in the contracting process is to identify the day-to-day situations that are made more difficult because of OCD and accommodating behaviors. This helps to establish problem areas that can be addressed through contracting. You can discover these problem areas by completing the self-monitoring logs and charts introduced in chapter 7.

Assessment of Accommodating Behaviors

After Alisha completed the self-monitoring exercises, she and Deon discussed what she had learned about her role in accommodating Deon's OCD. They agreed that Alisha's participation in Deon's checking rituals and her regular reassurance that all the rooms had been checked adequately were her primary accommodating behaviors.

Deon and Alisha could more easily identify recurring problematic situations and areas for change. They reviewed the Accommodating Behavior Log, discussed challenging situations, and agreed on the first problem area to address with the contracting process. They decided to work on the problematic situation of leaving the house together for short periods of time.

Identify the Long-Term Goal

Now that they had agreed upon the specific problem area to be addressed, they were ready to identify the related long-term goal: for Alisha to eliminate her participation in Deon's checking rituals and to refrain from reassuring Deon that he or they had checked adequately. Instead, she would encourage Deon to take risks by engaging in exposures.

Create Short-Term Goals

Next, they broke down their long-term goal into several smaller steps, or short-term goals. They made sure that with each progressive short-term goal, they were feeding the OCD less and less. A review of Alisha's accommodating log revealed that she had been completing approximately 50 percent of the checking when leaving for short outings together (in these situations, Alisha had assumed responsibility for checking the five upstairs rooms while Deon had been checking the downstairs rooms himself). Furthermore, she responded to Deon's requests for reassurance after leaving the home each time he asked, which could be as many as nine or ten times while on a short outing together.

As you can see in the contract, with each passing week, Alisha's short-term goals reflected less and less involvement in checking and reassuring. The couple agreed upon how to decrease her participation in checking rituals over the upcoming weeks and also agreed on an alternative response to Deon's requests for reassurance. Deon then assigned an anxiety level to each of the short-term goals as a means of gauging the anticipated distress associated with each short-term goal. In order to ensure adequate practice of their contract, they agreed to go on a short outing together (approximately forty-five minutes) at least once each day.

Identify Rewards

As a last step, Alisha and Deon identified rewards for their successful completion of long-term and short-term goals. Remember that it's important to recognize your and your loved one's efforts in making these difficult changes and paving the way for a life free from OCD. Alisha and Deon decided on a celebratory dinner at their favorite, yet expensive, restaurant as a reward for achieving their long-term goal. For meeting short-term goals, they rewarded themselves with specially planned weekend dates. They each contributed to a wish list of date ideas and took turns choosing a date from the list each week.

Alisha and Deon's Contract

Today's date: _January 1_   Target date: _February 11_

Problem: _In an effort to decrease Deon's anxiety and his time spent on rituals, Alisha checked the upstairs rooms for Deon before they left the house together. She also offered reassurance repeatedly after leaving home._

Long-term goal: _Alisha will eliminate her participation in checking rituals before leaving and will eliminate reassurance afterward. Deon will work individually with his therapist on ERP goals that will support their successful completion of the contract._

Reward: _A celebratory dinner at their favorite restaurant_

Short-term goal 1: _Alisha and Deon will leave the house together for a minimum of forty-five minutes at least once a day for the next seven days. Alisha will decrease checking to include only four rooms upstairs. She will limit providing reassurance to three times and then state the alternative response._

Anxiety level: _35_   When/frequency: _at least once daily_

Target date: _January 1-7_   Date completed: _____

Refrain from: *Alisha will refrain from checking all five rooms upstairs and from providing reassurance to Deon more than three times.*

Respond alternatively with: *Alisha will check only four upstairs rooms. When Deon asks for reassurance more than three times, Alisha will respond with, "We may or may not have checked enough times, and maybe we overlooked something that we would usually have shut off. We decided not to feed OCD anymore, and we can take the risk together. We'll deal with the possibility that the house is burning down only if and when it happens."*

Reward: *Alisha and Deon will praise and congratulate each other each night after successfully fulfilling their part of the contract. If the goal is successfully completed each day, then Deon will choose a date for the weekend from their wish list.*

Short-term goal 2: *Alisha and Deon will leave the house together for a minimum of forty-five minutes at least once a day for the next seven days. Alisha will decrease checking to include only three rooms upstairs. She will limit providing reassurance to two times and then state the alternative response.*

Anxiety level: *45*   When/frequency: *at least once daily*

Target date: *January 8-14*   Date completed: _____

Refrain from: *Alisha will refrain from checking all five rooms upstairs and from providing reassurance to Deon more than two times.*

Respond alternatively with: *Alisha will check only three upstairs rooms. If Deon asks for reassurance more than two times, Alisha will respond with, "We may or may not have checked enough times, and maybe we overlooked something that we would usually have shut off. We decided not to feed OCD anymore, and we can take the risk together. We'll deal with the possibility that the house is burning down only if and when it happens."*

Reward: *Alisha and Deon will praise and congratulate each other each night after successfully fulfilling their part of the contract. If the goal is successfully completed each day, then Alisha will choose a date for the weekend from their wish list.*

Short-term goal 3: *Alisha and Deon will leave the house together for a minimum of forty-five minutes at least once a day for the next seven days. Alisha will decrease checking to include only two rooms upstairs. She will limit providing reassurance to one time and then state the alternative response.*

Anxiety level: *50*   When/frequency: *at least once daily*

Target date: __*January 15-21*__   Date completed: _____

Refrain from: __*Alisha will refrain from checking all five rooms upstairs and from providing*__ __*reassurance to Deon more than one time.*__

Respond alternatively with: __*Alisha will check only two upstairs rooms. If Deon asks for*__ __*reassurance more than one time, Alisha will respond with, "We may or may not have*__ __*checked enough times, and maybe we overlooked something that we would usually have shut*__ __*off. We decided not to feed OCD anymore, and we can take the risk together. We'll deal*__ __*with the possibility that the house is burning down only if and when it happens."*__

Reward: __*Alisha and Deon will praise and congratulate each other each night after*__ __*successfully fulfilling their part of the contract. If the goal is successfully completed each day,*__ __*then Deon will choose a date for the weekend from their wish list.*__

Short-term goal 4: __*Alisha and Deon will leave the house together for a minimum of*__ __*forty-five minutes at least one time each day for the next seven days. Alisha will decrease*__ __*checking to include only one room upstairs. She will limit providing reassurance to one time*__ __*and then state the alternative response.*__

Anxiety level: __60__   When/frequency: __*at least once daily*__

Target date: __*January 22-28*__   Date completed: _____

Refrain from: __*Alisha will refrain from checking all five rooms upstairs and from providing*__ __*reassurance to Deon more than one time.*__

Respond alternatively with: __*Alisha will check only one upstairs room. If Deon asks for*__ __*reassurance more than one time, Alisha will respond with, "We may or may not have*__ __*checked enough times, and maybe we overlooked something that we would usually have shut*__ __*off. We decided not to feed OCD anymore, and we can take the risk together. We'll deal*__ __*with the possibility that the house is burning down only if and when it happens."*__

Reward: __*Alisha and Deon will praise and congratulate each other each night after*__ __*successfully fulfilling their part of the contract. If the goal is successfully completed each day,*__ __*then Alisha will choose a date for the weekend from their wish list.*__

Short-term goal 5: __*Alisha and Deon will leave the house together for a minimum of*__ __*forty-five minutes at least one time each day for the next seven days. Alisha will check none*__ __*of the five rooms upstairs. She will limit providing reassurance to one time and then state the*__ __*alternative response.*__

Anxiety level: ___70___   When/frequency: __*at least once daily*__

Target date: __*January 29-February 4*__   Date completed: _____

Refrain from: ___*Alisha will refrain from checking any of the five rooms upstairs and from*___ __*providing reassurance to Deon more than one time.*_____

Respond alternatively with: ___*Alisha will check none of the five upstairs rooms. If and when*___ *Deon asks for reassurance more than one time, Alisha will respond with, "We may or may* *not have checked enough times, and maybe we overlooked something that we would usually* *have shut off. We decided not to feed OCD anymore, and we can take the risk together.* *We'll deal with the possibility that the house is burning down only if and when it happens."*

Reward: ___*Alisha and Deon will praise and congratulate each other each night after*___ *successfully fulfilling their part of the contract. If the goal is successfully completed each day,* *then Deon will choose a date for the weekend from their wish list.*

Short-term goal 6: ___*Alisha and Deon will leave the house together for a minimum of 45*___ *minutes at least one time each day for the next seven days. Alisha will check none of the five* *rooms upstairs and she will refrain from providing any form of reassurance to Deon. If Deon* *asks for reassurance, she will state the alternative response.*

Anxiety level: ___75___   When/frequency: __*at least once daily*__

Target date: __*February 5-11*__   Date completed: _____

Refrain from: ___*Alisha will refrain from checking any of the five rooms upstairs and from*___ *providing any form of reassurance to Deon.*

Respond alternatively with: ___*Alisha will check none of the five upstairs rooms. If and*___ *when Deon asks for reassurance, Alisha will respond with, "We may or may not have* *checked enough times, and maybe we overlooked something that we would usually have shut* *off. We decided not to feed OCD anymore, and we can take the risk together. We'll deal* *with the possibility that the house is burning down only if and when it happens."*

Reward: ___*Alisha and Deon will praise and congratulate each other each night after*___ *successfully fulfilling their part of the contract. If the goal is successfully completed each day,* *then Deon and Alisha will have a special dinner date at their favorite restaurant.*

Signature: __*Alisha*_____

Signature: __*Deon*_____

ADJUSTING TO LIFE IN THE AFTERMATH OF OCD

As you and your spouse recover from OCD, you may experience further challenges associated with the changing roles and responsibilities in your relationship. For your spouse, reestablishing balance may involve assuming previously held spousal and household responsibilities and renegotiating decision-making roles within your marriage. It may also involve adjusting to and applying a newly developed sense of independence from reliance upon others, including you.

As the supportive spouse, reestablishing balance could mean surrendering previously held responsibilities, which may make you fearful or anxious. This may be especially true if you were significantly depended on for accommodations and enabling. Despite the relief you may experience in the short term, you might find that your spouse's newly developing sense of strength and independence functions as a threat to your own sense of usefulness and self-worth. After all, your role in supporting your spouse through OCD helped to establish an unwritten agreement about roles within the marriage. Feelings such as these may be considered normal given the history of the relationship, but they may in turn threaten further recovery from OCD. This is especially likely if you don't communicate what you're feeling. When feelings are left unresolved, they can inadvertently undermine your ability to be supportive of your spouse's recovery.

As you and your spouse continue on the road to recovery, your roles will need to be reestablished and redefined over and over again. You are on a journey with your spouse that can strengthen your connection and bring you closer in ways that feel refreshing and healthy.

Summary

It's important to consider yourself a partner in your spouse's battle against OCD. Joining together to fight OCD will build resiliency and strengthen trust and emotional intimacy within your marriage. Discuss with your spouse how OCD has interfered with your relationship emotionally, physically, financially, and socially. What effect does OCD have on your roles within your relationship? Agree on a particular problem you'd like to resolve, and then use the contracting process to bring about changes that will help you run OCD out of your marriage.

Chapter 10

Building Family Resilience

Resilience is the ability to withstand challenges, adversity, and stress. There are things you and your family can do to build resilience that will help you confront OCD and other difficulties that threaten your family. We all face challenges and adversity. As you read this chapter, examine how prepared you and your family are to deal with illness and other difficulties. Make note of positive changes you can make to build family resilience. Don't be overwhelmed, though—even small changes can make a difference. Start with a few positive changes. When you see the difference, you'll be inspired to make further changes.

TAKE CARE OF YOUR BODY

Anything that involves change can be stressful. Illness in the family, changes in work schedules, facing the challenges of cognitive behavioral therapy, and making changes in the way you respond to OCD are all possible sources of stress. Facing stressful situations for long periods can take a toll on your body and contribute to a variety of physical ailments, including heart disease, high blood pressure, diabetes, headaches, ulcers, chronic diarrhea, and muscle tension.

An important part of reducing stress and building resilience is taking care of your physical body. You can build your resilience in three major areas: through a stress-reducing diet, with exercise, and by getting adequate sleep. At first, changes in your diet and exercise level, or even trying to get more sleep, may seem anxiety provoking, rather than anxiety relieving. This is especially true if you are a perfectionist and tend to try to make major changes overnight. Our advice is to make one or two changes at a time. A stress-reducing diet is a well-balanced diet. The following are some suggestions for a well-balanced diet:

- Eat plenty of fruits and vegetables.

- Replace refined carbohydrates, such as white bread, pasta, potato chips, cakes, pies, and candy, with complex carbohydrates, such as whole grain breads and cereals, brown rice, and vegetables.

- Reduce saturated animal fats. Better sources of fat are monounsaturated oils, such as olive and canola oils.

- Eat plenty of fish, nuts, beans, soy products, and legumes.

- Avoid caffeine (coffee, tea, soda, chocolate, some over-the-counter medications). The stimulating effect of caffeine can have the same effects as stress on your body. Caffeine can result in restlessness, irritability, and difficulty sleeping. You may want to taper off gradually, since abrupt withdrawal can cause headaches, fatigue, and depression.

- Avoid nicotine. Smoking may seem relaxing, but nicotine is a stimulant, so it is actually stressful. In the short term, quitting may seem stressful, but the long-term result is stress reduction.

Alisha found her own anxiety increasing as she worried about her husband Deon's OCD. She had been taking on more and more responsibility because Deon had so much difficulty leaving the house without checking his computer and all the lights and appliances. It was easier for her to take on the responsibility of checking everything, then checking the door when they left the house together. She rearranged her work schedule so she could leave for work after him, promising to check everything as he had directed.

When Deon began ERP and they developed a family contract, Alisha looked at her own life. Besides decreasing and then ending her accommodating behaviors, Alisha could see things she could do to decrease her own anxiety. She gradually cut down and then stopped drinking coffee, and was amazed at the tension relief this produced. Together, the couple planned meals that were well-balanced and stress reducing. They joined a gym and developed exercise programs. In addition to reducing stress, they both lost weight and felt more energized and confident about reaching other goals. Deon and Alisha found that they enjoyed working as a team on improving their health, as well as beating the OCD.

Physical exercise builds resilience by enhancing our sense of well-being. It stimulates the production of endorphins, natural pain-reducing and mood-moderating chemicals. Exercise also enhances oxygenation of the blood and brain, which improves concentration, memory, and alertness, improves digestion, reduces blood pressure, and reduces muscle tension. Aerobic exercise is best for improving cardiovascular fitness, reducing stress and anxiety, and relieving muscle tension. It raises your heart rate and increases the efficiency of oxygen intake by the body. Aerobic exercise includes swimming, cycling, stationary biking, brisk walking, running, and vigorous dancing. Anaerobic exercise, such as short-distance swimming, sprinting, or weight lifting, is also helpful. It involves short bursts of activity and builds muscle.

Set a goal of exercising four to five times a week for twenty to thirty minutes. Don't worry if you miss a day or even a week. Exercise to reduce stress, not to add stress to your life! Cherry and her husband Jim have a goal of exercising two to four times a week. They go to the gym when he gets home from work. Since their goal is only two to four days a week, it's an easy goal to meet, even if something interferes with the schedule. When one of them is sick, they're on vacation, or company is in town, they don't go to the gym. In the past, this would have been the end of any exercise program for them. Now, even if it's been two weeks since they've been to the gym, they'll go back. As a result, they've been visiting the gym, usually only walking briskly on the treadmill, for the last five years.

Your body also needs rest. Inadequate sleep causes anxiety and stress, and this makes it even more difficult to sleep, creating a cycle of poor sleep habits. Adequate sleep will build your resilience and help you withstand the challenges of life. Are you getting enough sleep? If the answer is yes to any of the following questions, you may not be getting enough sleep:

- Do you often wake up tired?

- In the mornings, do you punch the snooze button on your alarm clock, sometimes more than once?

- Are you not as alert as you think you should be?

- Are you tired or sleepy during the day?

- Do you have an overwhelming desire to take a nap during the day?

If you find that you do need more sleep, try to develop a regular sleep schedule by going to bed and getting up at the same time each day. Pay attention to what your body is telling you. If you're tired, go to bed. Be respectful of the sleep needs of other family members, as well. When Jim's work schedule changed, he had to get up an hour earlier. Night after night, Cherry continued to encourage him to stay up until 11:00 P.M. Finally, they both realized that Jim needed to go to bed an hour earlier. She had been inadvertently interfering with his sleep schedule. Remember, the goal is building *family resilience*, not just individual resilience.

Are you still indulging in caffeine? Avoiding it in the evening will help you sleep. It's also best to stay away from alcoholic beverages at night. Contrary to many people's beliefs, alcohol actually disrupts sleep patterns. Arrange your bedroom so that it induces sleep by reducing noise and light. Make sure your bed and pillows are comfortable. Reducing activity and developing a relaxing routine at bedtime will help you sleep. Regular exercise improves sleep, but make certain it's a few hours before bedtime. If you can't sleep once you do go to bed, get up and do something relaxing in another room.

List three changes you will make to help you care for your body and build your resilience on the Care for Your Body chart. You may want to make copies for other family members and discuss your answers.

Care for Your Body

List three changes you will make to help you care for your body and build your resilience.

1. _____

_____

2. _____

_____

3. _____

_____

TAKE CARE OF YOUR MIND

How you look at the world and interpret events affects your resilience. In their book, *The Resilience Factor*, Karen Reivich and Andrew Shatte (2002, 11) refer to this as *cognitive style*, or *thinking style*. *The Resilience Factor* is a good resource for helping to overcome weaknesses and build on strengths. The authors describe thinking traps that adversely affect people's ability to respond to the challenges of life. Learning not to jump to conclusions, overlook the big picture, assume what other people are thinking, blow things out of proportion, or minimize problems helps us to become more resilient. Learning to stop blaming ourselves for everything or, conversely, blaming others for our problems builds confidence, a sense of self-worth, and resilience.

Your loved one is challenging the obsessive thoughts and false beliefs of his or her OCD. Challenging our own false beliefs and the negative thoughts they cause can improve how we all handle daily stress. What one person considers extremely stressful may be considered only a slight challenge or perhaps even an opportunity by another person. What makes a situation stressful is our perception. It is stressful when we perceive a situation as a threat to our physical or psychological well-being and believe we can't cope with the threat. Since situations and events don't cause stress, the answer is not changing the circumstances, but changing our perceptions and our learned beliefs about them. Recognizing this will help you choose how you look at life. You'll be more resilient and able to handle stress.

When Alisha joined a support group, she witnessed how other family members were handling their loved one's OCD. A few members of the group seemed angry, defeated, and depressed. Others were optimistic, confident, and hopeful. They encouraged each other and shared information. While the first set viewed OCD as a devastating disease with little hope for recovery, the attitude of the more optimistic members was that OCD was just another illness that could be overcome. Alisha chose to perceive her situation in the more positive light, to consider Deon's OCD as a challenge that could bring them closer together as they fought against it.

The next time you face a stressful situation, step back and observe your negative thoughts. Are you falling into a thinking trap, blowing things out of proportion, or jumping to conclusions? Can you reframe the situation as a challenge or an opportunity for growth? If you look really hard, you might even be able to find the humor in the circumstances. How often have you been able to look back and laugh about things that seemed devastating at the time? Laugh now! Laughter can decrease stress, relieve anxiety, and give you a more positive perception of life.

List some positive changes you will make in the way you perceive life on the Care for Your Mind chart. You may want to make copies for other family members and discuss your answers.

Care for Your Mind

List three positive changes you will make in the way you perceive life.

1. _____

_____

2. _____

_____

3. _____

_____

TAKE CARE OF YOUR SPIRIT

Stress also takes a tremendous toll on our spirits. Daily renewal builds resilience. This is especially important when we're facing a stressful situation. Enduring the effects of OCD and struggling to fight the disorder is one of those stressful situations. It's important that you and every family member make time in your lives for rest, relaxation, recreation, outside support, and spiritual renewal.

Just as your body needs sleep, your mind and spirit need continual renewal. They need the rest that comes from relaxing and uplifting activities. You need to take time daily to renew your mind, body, and spirit, even if it's only a few minutes. Spend time reading, taking a warm bath, listening to pleasant music, meditating or praying, doing needlework, painting, or working in the garage. The possible activities are endless. If you're a spiritual person, maintaining and growing in your faith will help build your resilience. Like-minded people can also be a good source of support for you and your family. Cherry and Jim found much-needed support from their friends at church. Alisha found tremendous strength from her support group. Her family and friends were helpful, but she felt that only those who also had close family members with OCD could truly understand what she was going through. She developed friends from her group whom she could call on when she needed to be uplifted.

Daily rest isn't enough rest to build and maintain family and individual resilience. Take special time out every week for rest and recreation. And, periodically take a vacation. You may not be able to take a formal vacation because of finances or even because of the struggle with OCD. You might not even be able to leave town. But that doesn't have to keep you from taking a "vacation." Instead of expensive elaborate two-week trips that perhaps tire out everyone and cause *unrest* rather than *rest*, you could plan several long weekend trips every year, go camping close to home, spend several nights in a local motel, or go on a retreat. When Cherry's son came home from college for spring break, she took time off from her writing, Jim took several days off from work, and they had a mini vacation at home. They went to the movies and out to eat every day and spent time with their son whenever he wasn't out with his friends.

Even daily and weekly renewal and periodic vacations aren't always enough to build resilience. You need to be attentive to signs of stress in your body. Be ready to give yourself extra breaks. Learn a relaxation technique that you can practice at your desk or sitting on the couch. Take a short walk, play a computer game, play with your cat or your child. If you know certain times of the day are stressful, prepare for them by doing whatever works best to renew your spirit.

List some changes you will make to help periodically renew your spirit and build your resilience on the Care for Your Spirit chart. You may want to make copies for other family members and discuss your answers.

Care for Your Spirit

List three changes you will make to help periodically renew your spirit and build your resilience.

1. _____

   _____

2. _____

   _____

3. _____

   _____

MAKE PLANS FOR MEETING YOUR GOALS

Working as a family and meeting together builds resilience by helping family members see themselves as a team. Meeting your goals builds individual and family confidence and resilience. Discuss the desired changes you've listed in this chapter in your family meetings and consider incorporating some of them as goals in your family contracts. Encourage other family members to discover ways to build resilience by caring for their bodies, minds, and spirits too.

What if things just don't seem to be working? You're not meeting your goals. Your loved one doesn't seem motivated or isn't meeting his or her goals. The question isn't "What if?" but "When?" The best preparation is to be aware that setbacks can happen and that your family is not alone. For most families, the OCD struggle is like a roller coaster, with highs and lows; the highs eventually become more frequent and the lows less frequent and not quite so low. Resilience means persevering and keeping up hope in the face of adversity. If something isn't working, examine your goals and plans in your family meetings and make new goals. No blame should be cast. Remind all family members that OCD is a long-term struggle.

Summary

Everyone has problems to deal with. These problems can help build resilience and prepare us for the next challenge. Often, families become stronger because of shared experiences. It can break you or make you stronger. You have a choice. Make resilience and strength your choice. Caring for your mind, body, and spirit will make you a more resilient individual and family that is stronger and more able to weather storms. Include caring for your mind, body, and spirit in the goals you and your family set for yourselves.

Chapter 11

Looking to the Future

Reading this workbook has hopefully been a source of encouragement for you. It probably hasn't solved all your OCD problems. If you just finished reading this book, it's doubtful that you've *solved* very many problems. If you've followed the plans in this book, your major accomplishments in these early days and weeks have been

- Gathering information

- Discovering where to find further information

- Negotiating a contract with your loved one

- Beginning the implementation of a contract with your loved one

- Nurturing hope for your loved one's and your family's future

You'll see results that are more tangible many months from now, once you've implemented what you've learned in this book. This chapter will discuss the many issues that can complicate recovery from OCD. When a person has other illnesses along with OCD, the treatment may need to be adjusted. Since obsessive-compulsive disorder can be a genetic disorder, it is common for more than one family member to have OCD, which can cause complications in treatment and family support. Your loved one may not yet be receiving treatment or not even be diagnosed yet. You may be questioning if the treatment is the best choice. Perhaps the most difficult issue to deal with is when a loved one refuses to get help. This chapter will cover all of these topics.

COMPLICATION WITH OTHER DISORDERS

The treatment of OCD can be quite challenging when a person has another illness. Other psychiatric disorders have symptoms such as intrusive thoughts, repetitive behaviors, and anxiety that make them very similar to OCD. Many people who suffer from these disorders try to resist the behaviors and find their lives greatly disrupted by their symptoms. Because they seem so closely related to OCD, these disorders are known as *obsessive-compulsive spectrum disorders*, or OCSDs. These disorders seem to have some biological similarities. They respond to the same group of antidepressants as OCD, selective serotonin reuptake inhibitors, and they appear to have higher than normal levels of activity in the frontal lobes of the brain (Penzel 2000). Included in this group of disorders are body dysmorphic disorder, trichotillomania, compulsive skin picking and nail biting, Tourette's syndrome, and some eating disorders.

People with body dysmorphic disorder (BDD) have a preoccupation, or obsession, with an imagined or minor defect in their appearance. Their compulsions can include frequently checking their appearance, trying to cover up imagined or minor defects, skin picking to "fix" flaws, seeking reassurance about their appearance from others, and seeking and receiving medical and cosmetic treatments. Like people with OCD, their lives are significantly impaired by their illness.

People with trichotillomania (TTM) compulsively pull their bodily hair. They may pull their hair from any part of the body, including the scalp, eyelashes, eyebrows, arms, underarm area, legs, and pubic area. For some people, hair pulling is preceded by an increasing sense of tension. For others it seems automatic; they may not even be aware that they are pulling their hair. Similar to OCD or BDD, hair pulling can be part of a ritual—pulling hairs to somehow make things even or to improve appearance. Unlike OCD, hair pulling can bring short-term pleasure or relaxation.

Compulsive skin picking and nail biting are not included in the *DSM-IV-TR* (APA 2000) as official disorders, but they are considered to be OCSDs. People can pick at their skin to the point of having open sores and then pick the resulting scabs. Some people, like those with BDD, pick with a goal of making a blemish look better. They may even examine their skin, looking for imperfect spots that need to be picked or made more perfect looking. Indeed, they may have BDD, with skin picking as a complication. Others pick at their skin in response to an urge. Nail biting can also be quite severe and can include biting and picking at cuticles. Again, unlike OCD, skin picking and nail biting can seem to reduce tension or be relaxing.

Tourette's syndrome is characterized by both vocal and motor tics, involuntary behaviors that are done in response to an urge or feeling of discomfort. Tics are less voluntary than the rituals of OCD. Typically, a person can postpone tics for a time but can't completely stop them. Tics don't seem to be driven by the need to relieve anxiety or by pleasure. People with Tourette's syndrome are more likely to have OCD than the general population. When a person has both OCD and Tourette's syndrome, during treatment it becomes necessary to distinguish between tics and rituals.

The treatment of BDD is similar to that of OCD. There may be more emphasis on raising self-esteem and treating depression. If skin picking is a problem, habit-reversal training can be an important part of treatment. Habit-reversal training is a self-management behavioral treatment that focuses on self-awareness, self-monitoring, and learning new habits that conflict with the negative behavior. Habit-reversal training is the main component of treatment plans for TTM, skin picking, and nail biting. Helpful resources for people with BDD, TTM, and habit disorders, including skin picking and nail biting, are included in the resources section at the end of this book.

Comorbid Disorders

Other disorders are not related, but are often seen together. These are known as *comorbid disorders*. Studies have shown that about 60 percent of people with OCD also have depression (Penzel 2000). It can be a result of having OCD, a part of the disorder, or a separate biological condition. Clinical depression and OCD both appear to be partly caused by a disturbance of the neurotransmitter serotonin, and they respond to the same medications. This suggests a possible link between the two disorders. Depression is characterized by hopelessness, helplessness, strong persistent feelings of sadness, loss of interest in normal activities and pursuits, lack of energy, impaired sleep and appetite, and, frequently, suicidal feelings.

The presence of depression greatly interferes with the treatment of OCD. It's difficult to make changes or concentrate on treatment objectives when feeling hopeless about the future. Your loved one may lack the energy to carry out plans and may have problems learning and remembering details. If your loved one is depressed, encourage him or her to seek treatment so that you'll both be better prepared to fight the OCD. Likewise, if you are depressed, seek help from a licensed mental-health professional. Most importantly, take talk or thoughts of suicide seriously. If your loved one talks about having thoughts of suicide or threatens to commit suicide, seek help from a qualified mental-health professional *immediately*. Most towns have a suicide hotline that can help you obtain appropriate help.

Comorbid disorders or the addition of another obsessive-compulsive spectrum disorder can complicate the treatment of OCD. Having another physical illness, such as asthma, diabetes, or heart disease, can also complicate matters. Your loved one may even need to have more than one health-care professional involved. You can meet the challenge by discovering as much as you can about each diagnosis and learning how you can best provide support.

When More Than One Family Member Has an Illness

It is quite likely that more than one person in your family has an OCD-related illness. OCD runs in families, so it is not uncommon for a parent and one or more children to have OCD. Recent studies showed that immediate family members of people with OCD in the studies had a 10.3 percent and 11.7 percent chance of having OCD compared to 1.9 percent and 2.7 percent of relatives in the control families (Rosario-Campos 2003). In addition, people with OCD appear to be more likely than members of the general population to have family members with OCSDs, depression, and other anxiety disorders. It is believed that both genetic and environmental factors play a role.

This may seem like bad news, but if you examine the facts more closely, you can see how it can be an advantage. If a certain number of people in the world are going to have OCD, why not place them in families where they can understand each other? If your family has more than one member with OCD or a related illness, view this as a naturally occurring support group or mentoring relationship. People with OCD can understand each other and support each other in ways that no one else can. Those with other OCSDs, depression, and other anxiety disorders may not be able to understand the torture of obsessions or the urge to ritualize quite as well, but they have an advantage over those without disorders. They've been touched by similar fears, anxieties, and worries. They've experienced similar disruptions in their relationships, and perhaps isolation because of their illness.

Maybe other family members don't have psychiatric disorders, but they have asthma, diabetes, heart disease, or cancer. The list is endless. Even with seemingly unrelated illnesses, you can find common ground. When Cherry was diagnosed with OCD, she better understood her Aunt Margaret, who had been diagnosed with diabetes at the age of nineteen, when insulin was first developed. Her aunt lived her life according to strict rules, weighing her food, walking daily, always alert for signs of high or low blood sugar. Because she cared for her body and was so determined to live victoriously with her illness, Aunt Margaret lived to the age of ninety and died with no diabetic complications. Cherry was inspired to make major changes in her life to gain victory, just as her aunt had.

Joan's father, Robert, had received treatment for OCD and appeared to be nearly symptom free when his daughter was diagnosed with OCD. But when she began treatment, they discovered that his responses to Joan's OCD were having a negative impact. For example, he reassured her that there was nothing to worry about when she obsessed over causing harm. Often, he became caught up in her obsessive worries and even urged her to check things out "just to make sure things are fine." When Joan started therapy and developed exposure exercises, Robert found that he couldn't offer the kind of support she needed. He sometimes even interfered with exposures, afraid she might be doing something that would cause too much anxiety. Robert finally realized that his own OCD was out of control. Reassuring Joan and participating in her rituals had become rituals for him too. He set up a plan for tackling his fears with exposure and ritual prevention exercises. Together, Robert and Joan used contracting to fight their OCD and won.

FINDING HELP

It's important to learn what you can about OCD so that you can offer the best support to your loved one as possible. You can help by sharing information about OCD and the resources available. You'll want to be prepared to point your loved one in the right direction. If he or she is already receiving treatment, you'll want to be able to help evaluate how the treatment is working.

People with mild to moderate OCD can use a self-directed approach to cognitive behavioral therapy. If your loved one is considering a self-directed approach, he or she should consult with a mental-health professional first. It's important to make certain you have an accurate diagnosis and to rule out other illnesses. There would then be someone to turn to if medication or more extensive therapy is needed. Even with mild OCD, it's a good idea to start out with a therapist before embarking on a self-directed plan. When OCD is severe or when it is complicated by depression or other disorders, professional help is certainly needed.

Your loved one may not have come to the point of recognizing a need for help. In this case, your first step is to gather information about OCD and the resources available in your community. Then you will want to arrange a comfortable time to discuss your concerns, either individually or as a family. Try to neither minimize nor overdramatize the problems. Demonstrate your acceptance of the illness and interest in the difficulties your loved one is experiencing. Help your loved one to understand that this is just one more challenge for your family, something that together you can overcome. Remind each other of other difficulties you've faced and other illnesses your family has had to deal with. It helps to regard OCD as an illness, not a weakness. Discuss the *possibility* of OCD; let the doctor do the diagnosing. This will make the discussion less threatening.

HOW TO FIND A THERAPIST

Perhaps your loved one recognizes there's a problem and would like your assistance finding appropriate treatment. How do you find help? The first person to ask is your family physician. Some doctors are knowledgeable enough about OCD to prescribe medication if it is needed. He or she also may be able to refer you to a mental-health professional. Family physicians are in a good position to know where to get the best treatment. They refer patients and then get feedback about the results. Your insurance might also require that you go through your family doctor for a referral to a specialist.

It's important that your therapist or doctor be experienced in the treatment of OCD. The Obsessive-Compulsive Foundation (OCF), Obsessive Compulsive Information Center (Dean Foundation), Association for Advancement of Behavior Therapy (AABT), and Anxiety Disorders Association of America (ADAA) all maintain lists of mental-health professionals who have identified themselves as professionals treating OCD. (Contact information for these organizations is listed in the resources section at the end of this book.) Since those listing themselves are only self-identified as experts, you will still need to check out their qualifications. You can do so by contacting the state licensing board for a particular clinician's profession (medicine, psychology, social work). You can reach these state licensing boards by calling your state government general information line.

Psychiatrists can prescribe medications, but don't usually provide cognitive behavioral therapy. Some have sought additional training and do provide CBT, while others work closely with therapists who do. It is essential that your loved one's psychiatrist be willing to support CBT. If you find a psychiatrist first, he or she may be able to refer you to a psychologist or counselor who is trained to treat OCD using ERP.

How to Evaluate a Therapist

Your loved one may be starting treatment, and you're both wondering if it's the right treatment. Initial information can easily be obtained before making the first appointment. Make certain that potential therapists are licensed by the state. On the telephone, ask therapists or their representatives about their experience treating people with OCD.

Questions to Ask Therapists

- What techniques do they use? The answer you want to hear is cognitive behavioral therapy, behavioral therapy, or behavior therapy. Ask what kind of behavior therapy they use. *Exposure and ritual prevention* (sometimes called *exposure and response prevention*) is an essential part of the treatment of OCD. If ERP isn't used, you probably want to look for treatment elsewhere.

- What kind of training has the therapist received? Look for training in cognitive behavioral therapy of anxiety disorders.

- How many patients has the therapist treated for OCD? The perfect scenario would be finding a therapist who specializes in treating anxiety disorders, including OCD. This therapist would be someone your loved one feels comfortable with in a short period of time. Experience is an important qualification, but don't waste time looking for the *perfect* therapist.

- If necessary, will the therapist assist in ERP exercises outside the office? Is the therapist willing to help the person get started and then assist in self-directed ERP?

- How much of a role do family members play in the treatment process? Are there support groups available for family members?

- Is the therapist available between sessions? Is there a number to call for emergencies?

Before treatment can begin, the therapist will spend two or three sessions doing a thorough assessment. This will establish that OCD is indeed the problem and will determine how OCD affects your loved one's life. The therapist will probably administer a Yale-Brown Obsessive Compulsive Scale (YBOCS) to measure the severity of OCD symptoms. This will provide more information about the frequency, intensity, and duration of obsessions and compulsions, triggering situations, avoidance behaviors, and family involvement in OCD symptoms. The therapist can then administer a YBOCS periodically throughout treatment to measure your loved one's progress.

After assessing OCD symptoms, the therapist will discuss the treatment plan. Exposure and ritual prevention should be the focus. The therapist will help your loved one develop a hierarchy of fears, listing them from least anxiety provoking to most anxiety provoking. Then a plan will be produced for implementing ERP exercises: exposure to the fears while resisting the usual rituals. Although some exercises may be done in the office, most ERP exercises will be done at home. This is the homework. During therapy sessions, ERP exercises are discussed and new ones are planned. The therapist will also teach cognitive strategies that are aimed at confronting the distorted thoughts and beliefs that sustain the rituals.

This form of cognitive behavioral therapy is the most effective treatment of OCD. There may also be a need for family or marital therapy to address other problems.

What If a Qualified Therapist Is Not Available?

What if your loved one can't find a therapist who is experienced in the treatment of OCD? In many areas, there is a shortage of qualified OCD therapists. Consider venturing outside of your community to obtain treatment. This could mean traveling several hours to therapy sessions or checking into an intensive inpatient or outpatient OCD program. The Obsessive-Compulsive Foundation keeps a list of such programs. Another option is purchasing a self-help book, such as *The OCD Workbook* (Hyman and Pedrick 1999), and having a therapist who is not experienced with OCD function as a coach. Then you can encourage the therapist to seek further training. Contact the OCF about educational opportunities for professionals. It periodically conducts the Behavior Therapy Institute (BTI), a three-day intensive training for the treatment of OCD for mental-health professionals throughout the country.

What If Your Loved One Refuses Help?

One of the most difficult situations is living with OCD when a loved one refuses treatment or refuses to acknowledge there's a problem. Watching a loved one suffer while knowing there is help available can make you feel hopeless and even angry. There is reason to have hope for the future however. As you grow in your knowledge about OCD, your loved one will likely want to learn too. Share what you're learning. Make plans for gradually withdrawing reassurance and accommodation. Give your loved one a time line of when and how you will be doing so. Assure him or her that you are learning to respond in a more positive way to the OCD, and that you are doing it out of love.

Sandy had hoarding OCD. Her vast collection of magazines, books, and newspapers were stacked from floor to ceiling in every room of her house. She also took in homeless cats until she had almost one hundred living in and around her house. Sandy insisted she was helping the cats, but taking in cats she couldn't care for only kept them from finding other homes. Sandy lived alone and had few friends. Her brothers and sisters urged her to get help, but she refused to even admit that she had a problem. They also urged their sister Martha to stop helping financially with cat food. Martha was as exasperated as the rest of the family, but she found it difficult to see the cats going hungry. If Sandy wouldn't give up the cats, she reasoned, at least she could help feed them. When Martha stopped helping with the cat food, the situation deteriorated. Sandy continued to take in more cats, even though she couldn't feed them and there was no room in the house or the yard.

The neighbors complained about the smell produced by so many cats. The cats were also killing the neighborhood birds. Many of the cats were starving and scavenging from neighbors' garbage cans. A neighbor finally called animal control, which took the cats away. Then the health department found the home to be uninhabitable. Sandy had to move out of her house until the carpet was replaced and the house was professionally cleaned. The health department also advised her that the stacked newspapers and magazines were a fire hazard. She would need to rid her house of them. Again, Sandy's brothers and sisters urged her to get help. They presented the information they'd collected. This time, she took their advice and began a cognitive behavioral therapy program.

Withdrawal of reassurance and accommodation will likely produce anxiety in the short term. It could be a tumultuous time for the family, but the anxiety might be just what your loved one needs to finally become convinced of the need for help. Before you begin your plan for giving more positive support, provide information about the local resources you've learned about. Then be ready to assist in getting help when your loved one is ready.

What If Nothing Seems to Be Working?

Obsessive-compulsive disorder can be so severe that nothing seems to work. Melinda was still living with her parents at the age of fifty. The lives of both parents revolved around keeping Melinda's anxiety under control and assisting with her OCD rituals. Foods and cleaning supplies had to be purchased at a particular store. To get her to eat, her parents participated in elaborate counting rituals. She spent hours cleaning her room and bathroom. When her anxiety soared, Melinda's mother helped her clean, following her specific cleaning rules. Both parents had developed health problems and they worried about what would happen to Melinda when they died. She'd tried numerous medications and worked with every therapist within one hundred miles, but nothing seemed to help.

Melinda worried about her future too. She wanted to be free from OCD. After Melinda and her parents researched their options, Melinda enrolled in an inpatient treatment program. Her parents stayed with relatives and attended family support groups while she was in the program. They learned how to better support Melinda. At home, Melinda continued treatment with a local therapist. They used contracting to better manage OCD symptoms. A major goal was moving into an apartment and living independently. The family celebrated when she accomplished this. Her parents now visit daily and Melinda still calls frequently, but she is becoming more independent. They no longer fear for her future because they can see their daughter growing stronger every day.

SUPPORT GROUPS

In the process of reading this book, you've found that you are not alone in your struggle with OCD. Other families all over are dealing with the same things. Support groups can help your family cope with OCD. The Obsessive-Compulsive Foundation keeps a list of OCD-related support groups throughout the world. The foundation has made it easy to search for a local support group on its Web site.

The OCF also keeps a list of online support groups with instructions on how to join them. These are electronic mailing lists in which, after signing up, members receive emails from the entire group. You can then simply read the emails or reply to the group. There is also a large general electronic mailing list for discussing treatment options and how OCD affects lives, families, and relationships. There are also highly targeted smaller support lists that zero in on specific OCD needs, focusing on certain symptoms, family members, parents, teens, and children. There are even lists for cat and dog owners.

Summary

So often, we all do things without really knowing why we're doing them. As you've seen, this is common in families dealing with OCD. This book has provided tools to help your family break free from the oppression of OCD. It's time to develop a vision of life free of OCD for you, your loved one, and your family. Let that vision guide you and explain what you do. If other issues are complicating the journey toward recovery, approach them in the same way you have the OCD. Research other illnesses that your loved one or other family members might have and get the appropriate help.

Even when OCD is the only illness in the family, remember that you all need help and support. OCD is a disorder that affects the entire family. Reach out to others who have paved the road toward recovery and let them share their insights.

Resources

BOOKS FOR FAMILIES

C., Roy. 1993. *Obsessive Compulsive Disorder: A Survival Guide for Family and Friends.* New Hyde Park, N.Y.: Obsessive Compulsive Anonymous, Inc.

Gravitz, Herbert L. 1998. *Obsessive Compulsive Disorder: New Help for the Family.* Santa Barbara, Calif.: Healing Visions Press.

SELF-HELP BOOKS

Baer, Lee. 2001. *Getting Control: Overcoming Your Obsessions and Compulsions.* Rev. ed. New York: Plume.

Baer, Lee. 2002. *The Imp of the Mind: Exploring the Silent Epidemic of Obsessive Bad Thoughts.* New York: Plume.

C., Roy. 1999. *Obsessive Compulsive Anonymous: Recovering from Obsessive Compulsive Disorder.* 2nd ed. New Hyde Park, N.Y.: Obsessive Compulsive Anonymous, Inc.

Ciarrocchi, Joséph W. 1995. *The Doubting Disease: Help for Scrupulosity and Religious Compulsions.* Mahwah, N.J.: Paulist Press.

Crawford, Mark. 2004. *The Obsessive-Compulsive Trap.* Ventura, Calif.: Regal Books.

de Silva, Padmal, and Stanley Rachman. 1998. *Obsessive-Compulsive Disorder: The Facts.* 2nd ed. New York: Oxford University Press.

Dumont, Raeann. 1996. *The Sky Is Falling: Understanding and Coping with Phobias, Panic, and Obsessive-Compulsive Disorders.* New York: W. W. Norton.

Foa, Edna B., and Reid Wilson. 2001. *Stop Obsessing! How to Overcome Your Obsessions and Compulsions.* Rev. ed. New York: Bantam Books.

Grayson, Jonathan. 2003. *Freedom from Obsessive-Compulsive Disorder: A Personalized Recovery Program for Living with Uncertainty.* New York: Tarcher/Penguin Putnam.

Greist, John H. 1995. *Obsessive Compulsive Disorder: A Guide.* Madison, Wis.: Dean Foundation for Health, Research and Education.

Maran, Linda. 2004. *Confronting the Bully of OCD: Winning Back Our Freedom One Day at a Time.* New York: Fifteenth Street Publishing.

Munford, Paul R. 2004. *Overcoming Compulsive Checking: Free Your Mind from OCD.* Oakland, Calif.: New Harbinger Publications.

Neziroglu, Fugen, Jerome Bubrick, and José Yaryura-Tobias. 2004. *Overcoming Compulsive Hoarding: Why You Save and How You Can Stop.* Oakland, Calif.: New Harbinger Publications.

Neziroglu, Fugen, and José A. Yaryura-Tobias. 1997. *Over and Over Again: Understanding Obsessive-Compulsive Disorder.* Updated and Revised edition. Hoboken, N.J.: Jossey-Bass.

Osborn, Ian. 1999. *Tormenting Thoughts and Secret Rituals: The Hidden Epidemic of Obsessive-Compulsive Disorder.* New York: Dell Publishing Company.

Penzel, Fred. 2000. *Obsessive-Compulsive Disorders: A Complete Guide to Getting Well and Staying Well.* New York: Oxford University Press.

Rapoport, Judith L. 1997. *The Boy Who Couldn't Stop Washing: The Experience and Treatment of Obsessive-Compulsive Disorder.* New York: Signet Book.

Santa, Thomas. 1999. *Understanding Scrupulosity: Helpful Answers for Those Who Experience Nagging Questions and Doubts.* Liguori, Mo.: Liguori Publications.

Schwartz, Jeffrey, with Beverly Beyette. 1997. *Brain Lock: Free Yourself from Obsessive-Compulsive Behavior.* New York: Regan Books.

Steketee, Gail, and Kerin White. 1990. *When Once Is Not Enough: Help for Obsessive Compulsives.* Oakland, Calif.: New Harbinger Publications.

Van Noppen, Barbara L., Michele Tortora Pato, and Steven Rasmussen. 1997. *Learning to Live with OCD: Obsessive Compulsive Disorder.* 4th ed. Milford, Conn.: Obsessive-Compulsive Foundation.

BOOKS FOR PARENTS AND EDUCATORS

Adams, Gail B., and Marcia Torcia. 1998. *School Personnel: A Critical Link in the Identification, Treatment, and Management of OCD in Children and Adolescents*. Milford, Conn.: Obsessive-Compulsive Foundation.

Chansky, Tamar E. 2001. *Freeing Your Child from Obsessive-Compulsive Disorder: A Powerful, Practical Program for Parents of Children and Adolescents*. New York: Three Rivers Press.

———. 2004. *Freeing Your Child from Anxiety: Powerful, Practical Solutions to Overcome Your Child's Fears, Worries, and Phobias*. New York: Broadway Books.

Dornbush, Marilyn, and Sheryl Pruitt. 1995. *Teaching the Tiger: A Handbook for Individuals Involved in the Education of Students with Attention Deficit Disorders, Tourette's Syndrome or Obsessive-Compulsive Disorder*. Duarte, Calif.: Hope Press.

Fitzgibbons, Lee, and Cherry Pedrick. 2003. *Helping Your Child with OCD: A Workbook for Parents of Children with Obsessive-Compulsive Disorder*. Oakland, Calif.: New Harbinger Publications.

Greist, John H. 1993. *Obsessive-Compulsive Disorder in Children and Adolescents: A Guide*. Madison, Wis.: Dean Foundation for Health, Research and Education.

Johnston, Hugh F., and J. Jay Fruehling. *OCD and Parenting*. Madison, Wis.: Child Psychopharmacology Information Center, University of Wisconsin (Department of Psychiatry).

Swedo, Susan, and Henrietta Leonard. 1999. *Is It "Just a Phase"? How to Tell Common Childhood Phases from More Serious Problems*. New York: Broadway Books.

Wagner, Aureen Pinto. 2002. *What to Do When Your Child Has Obsessive-Compulsive Disorder: Strategies and Solutions*. Rochester, N.Y.: Lighthouse Press.

———. 2002. *Worried No More: Help and Hope for Anxious Children*. Rochester, N.Y.: Lighthouse Press.

BOOKS FOR CHILDREN AND TEENS

Harrar, George. 2003. *Not as Crazy as I Seem*. Boston, Mass.: Houghton Mifflin Company.

Hyman, Bruce M., and Cherry Pedrick. 2003. *Obsessive-Compulsive Disorder*. Brookfield, Conn.: Twenty-First Century Medical Library.

Niner, Holly L. 2004. *Mr. Worry: A Story about OCD*. Morton Grove, Ill.: Albert Whitman and Company.

Talley, Leslie. 2004. *A Thought Is Just a Thought*. New York: Lantern Books.

Vavrichek, Sherrie Mansfield, Ruth Goldfinger Golomb, and Uri Yokel. 2000. *The Hair Pulling "Habit" and You: How to Solve the Trichotillomania Puzzle.* Rev. ed. Silver Spring, Md.: Writers Cooperative of Greater Washington.

Wagner, Aureen Pinto. 2000. *Up and Down the Worry Hill.* Rochester, NY: Lighthouse Press.

PROFESSIONAL BOOKS

Clark, David A. 2004. *Cognitive-Behavioral Therapy for OCD.* New York: The Guilford Press.

Jenike, Michael A., Lee Baer, and William E. Minichiello, eds. 1998. *Obsessive-Compulsive Disorders: Practical Management.* 3rd ed. St. Louis, Mo.: Mosby, Inc.

March, John S., and Karen Mulle. 1998. *OCD in Children and Adolescents: A Cognitive-Behavioral Treatment Manual.* New York: The Guilford Press.

Steketee, Gail. 1999. *Overcoming Obsessive-Compulsive Disorder—Therapist Protocol (Best Practices Series).* Oakland, Calif.: New Harbinger Publications.

Yaryura-Tobias, José A., and Fugen Neziroglu. 1997. *Biobehavioral Treatment of Obsessive-Compulsive Spectrum Disorders.* New York: W. W. Norton.

BODY DYSMORPHIC DISORDER

Claiborn, James, and Cherry Pedrick. 2002. *The BDD Workbook: Overcome Body Dysmorphic Disorder and End Body Image Obsessions.* Oakland, Calif.: New Harbinger Publications.

Phillips, Katharine A. 1998. *The Broken Mirror: Understanding and Treating Body Dysmorphic Disorder.* New York: Oxford University Press.

TRICHOTILLOMANIA

Keuthen, Nancy J., Dan J. Stein, and Gary A. Christensen. 2001. *Help for Hair Pullers: Understanding and Coping with Trichotillomania.* Oakland, Calif.: New Harbinger Publications.

Penzel, Fred. 2003. *The Hair-Pulling Problem: A Complete Guide to Trichotillomania.* New York: Oxford University Press.

HABIT CHANGE

Claiborn, James, and Cherry Pedrick. 2000. *The Habit Change Workbook: How to Break Bad Habits and Form Good Ones*. Oakland, Calif.: New Harbinger Publications.

PROFESSIONAL JOURNAL ARTICLES

Chambless, Diane, Angela Bryan, Leona Aiken, Gail Steketee, and Jill Hooley. 1999. The structure of expressed emotion: A three-construct representation. *Psychological Assessment* 11(1):67-76.

Chambless, Diane, and Gail Steketee. 1999. Expressed emotion and behavior therapy outcome: A prospective study with obsessive-compulsive and agoraphobic outpatients. *Journal of Counseling and Clinical Psychology* 67(5):658-665.

Ginsburg, Golda, and Margaret Schlossberg. 2002. Family-based treatment of childhood anxiety disorders. *International Journal of Psychiatry* 14:142-153.

Ginsburg, Golda, Lynne Siqueland, Carrie Masia-Warner, and Kristina Hedtke. 2004. Anxiety disorders in children: Family matters. *Cognitive and Behavioral Practice* 11(1):28-43.

Ginsburg, Gail, Wendy Silverman, and William Kurtines. 1995. Family involvement in treating children with anxiety and phobic disorders: A look ahead. *Clinical Psychology Review* 15:457-473.

Steketee, Gail, and Barbara Van Noppen. 2003. Family approaches to treatment for obsessive compulsive disorder. *Journal of Family Psychotherapy* 14(4):43-50.

Van Noppen, Barbara. 1999. Multi-family behavioral treatment (MFBT) for OCD. *Crisis Intervention* 5(1-2):3-24.

Waters, Tracey, Paula Barrett, and John March. 2001. Cognitive-behavioral family treatment of childhood obsessive-compulsive disorder: Preliminary findings. *American Journal of Psychotherapy* 55(3):372-387.

MENTAL HEALTH ORGANIZATIONS AND WEB SITES

American Foundation for Suicide Prevention, 120 Wall Street, Twenty-second Floor, New York, NY 10005. (212) 363-3500. www.afsp.org.

Anxiety Disorders Association of America (ADAA), 8730 Georgia Avenue, Suite 600, Silver Spring, MD 20910. (240) 485-1001. www.adaa.org.

Association for the Advancement of Behavior Therapy, 305 Seventh Avenue, Sixteenth Floor, New York, NY 10001-6008. (212) 647-1890. www.aabt.org.

Attention Deficit Disorder Association (ADDA), P.O. Box 543, Pottstown, PA 19464. (484) 945-2101. www.add.org.

Awareness Foundation for OCD and Related Disorders. www.ocdawareness.com.

Cherry's Web site. CherryPedrick.com.

Children and Adults with Attention Deficit Disorders (CHADD), 8181 Professional Place, Suite 150, Landover, MD 20785. (800) 233-4050.

Consumer Website for Handling Your Mental Illness at Work and School, Center for Psychiatric Rehabilitation. www.bu.edu/sarpsych/jobschool.

Depression and Bipolar Support Alliance (DBSA). National Depressive and Manic-Depressive Association, 730 North Franklin, Suite 501, Chicago, IL 60610. (800) 82N-DMDA. www.dbsalliance.org.

Doubt and Other Disorders. www.healthyplace.com/communities/ocd/doubt.

Internet Mental Health. www.mentalhealth.com.

Internet Mental Health Infosource. www.mhsource.com.

National Alliance for the Mentally Ill, Colonial Place Three, 2107 Wilson Boulevard, Suite 300, Arlington, VA 22201-3042. (800) 950-6264. www.nami.org.

National Anxiety Foundation, 3135 Custer Drive, Lexington, KY 40517-4001. www.lexington-on-line.com/naf.

National Association of Anorexia Nervosa and Associated Disorders, Box 7, Highland Park, IL 60035. (847) 831-3438. www.anad.org.

National Eating Disorders Association, 603 Stewart Street, Seattle, WA 98101. (800) 931-2237. www.nationaleatingdisorders.org.

National Foundation for Depressive Illness, P.O. Box 2257, New York, NY 10116. (800) 239-1265. www.depression.org.

National Institute of Mental Health, Office of Communications, 6001 Executive Boulevard, Room 8184, MSC 9663, Bethesda, MD 20892-9663. (866) 615-6464. www.nimh.nih.gov.

National Mental Health Association, 2001 North Beauregard Street, Twelfth Floor, Alexandria, VA 22311. (703) 684-7722. www.nmha.org.

National Mental Health Consumers' Self-Help Clearinghouse, 1211 Chestnut Street, Suite 1207, Philadelphia, PA 19107. (800) 553-4539. www.mhselfhelp.org.

Obsessive Compulsive Anonymous (OCA), P.O. Box 215, New Hyde Park, NY 11040. (516) 739-0662. members.aol.com/west24th/index.html.

Obsessive-Compulsive Foundation (OCF), 676 State Street, New Haven, CT 06511. (203) 401-2070. www.ocfoundation.org.

Obsessive Compulsive Information Center, Madison Institute of Medicine, 7617 Mineral Point Road, Suite 300, Madison, WI 53717. (608) 827-2470. www.miminc.org/aboutocic.html.

OCD Action (OA; UK organization for people with OCD), Aberdeen Centre, 22-24 Highbury Grove, London, N5 2EA. +44 (0) 207-226-4000, Fax: +44 (0) 207-288-0828. www.ocdaction.org.uk.

OCD Online. www.ocdonline.com.

OCD Resource Center of South Florida. www.ocdhope.com.

Psych Central (Dr. John Grohol's mental health page). www.psychcentral.com.

Scrupulous Anonymous, Liguori Publications, One Liguori Drive, Liguori, MO 63057-9999. (800) 325-9521. mission.liguori.org/newsletters/scrupanon.htm.

Tourette Syndrome Association. 42-40 Bell Boulevard, Bayside, NY 11361-2820. (718) 224-2999. www.tsa-usa.org.

Trichotillomania Learning Center, 303 Potrero, Number 51, Santa Cruz, CA 95060. (831) 457-1004. www.trich.org.

References

Alsobrook, II, John P., and David L. Pauls. 1998. Genetics of obsessive-compulsive disorder. In *Obsessive-Compulsive Disorders: Practical Management*, 3rd ed., edited by Michael Jenike, Lee Baer, and William Minichiello. St. Louis, Mo.: Mosby, Inc.

American Psychiatric Association. 2000. *Diagnostic and Statistical Manual of Mental Disorders*. 4th ed. Text revision. Washington, D.C.: American Psychiatric Association.

Calvocoressi, Lisa, Barbara Lewis, Mary Harris, Sally J. Trufan, Wayne K. Goodman, Christopher McDougle, and Lawrence H. Price. 1995. Family accommodation in obsessive-compulsive disorder. *American Journal of Psychiatry* 152(3):441–443.

Geller, Daniel A. 1998. *Juvenile obsessive-compulsive disorder*. In *Obsessive-Compulsive Disorders: Practical Management*, 3rd ed., edited by Michael Jenike, Lee Baer, and William Minichiello. St. Louis, Mo.: Mosby, Inc.

Hyman, Bruce M., and Cherry Pedrick. 1999. *The OCD Workbook: Your Guide to Breaking Free from Obsessive-Compulsive Disorder*. Oakland, Calif.: New Harbinger Publications.

Jenike, Michael. 1998. Theories of etiology. In *Obsessive-Compulsive Disorders: Practical Management*, 3rd ed., edited by Michael Jenike, Lee Baer, and William Minichiello. St. Louis, Mo.: Mosby, Inc.

March, John S., and Karen Mulle. 1998. *OCD in Children and Adolescents: A Cognitive-Behavioral Treatment Manual*. New York: The Guilford Press.

Niehous, Dana J. H., and Dan J. Stein. 1997. Obsessive-compulsive disorder: Diagnosis and assessment. In *Obsessive-Compulsive Disorders: Diagnosis, Etiology, Treatment*, edited by Eric Hollander and Dan J. Stein. New York: Marcel Dekker, Inc.

Penzel, Fred. 2000. *Obsessive-Compulsive Disorders: A Complete Guide to Getting Well and Staying Well*. New York: Oxford University Press.

Reivich, Karen, and Andrew Shatte. 2002. *The Resilience Factor: Seven Essential Skills for Overcoming Life's Inevitable Obstacles*. New York: Broadway Books.

Rosario-Campos, Maria C. 2003. Genetic studies in obsessive-compulsive disorder. *OCD Newsletter* 7 (Winter).

Salkovskis, Paul. 1985. Obsessive-compulsive problems: A cognitive-behavioural analysis. *Behaviour Research and Therapy* 23:571–583.

Schwartz, Jeffery M., with Beverly Beyette. 1996. *Brain Lock: Free Yourself from Obsessive-Compulsive Disorder*. New York: HarperCollins.

Yaryura-Tobias, José A., and Fugen Neziroglu. 1997. *Biobehavioral Treatment of Obsessive-Compulsive Spectrum Disorders*. New York: W. W. Norton.